DR KATHERINE THOMPSON

AUSTRALIA'S CHRISTIAN
MINDFULNESS EXPERT

I0025885

THE
DISCIPLINE
OF SUFFERING

REDEEMING OUR STORIES OF PAIN

a. Acorn Press

Published by Acorn Press

An imprint of Bible Society Australia

ACN 148 058 306

GPO Box 4161

Sydney NSW 2001

Australia

www.acornpress.net.au | www.biblesociety.org.au

Charity licence 19 000 528

© Katherine Thompson 2023. All rights reserved.

ISBN: 9780647531792 (print); 9780647531808 (ebook)

A catalogue record for this book is available from the National Library of Australia

Apart from any fair dealing for the purposes of private study, research, criticism or review, no part of this work may be reproduced by electronic or other means without the permission of the publisher.

Katherine Thompson asserts her right under section 193 of the Copyright Act 1968 (Cth) to be identified as the author of this work.

Scripture quotations are taken from the Holy Bible, New International Version® Anglicized, NIV® Copyright © 1979, 1984, 2011 by Biblica, Inc.® Used by permission. All rights reserved worldwide.

Editor: Kristin Argall

Cover and text design and layout: Joy Lankshear

Contents

Acknowledgements

To my precious family and friends who have challenged me and pushed me to keep going through the toughest times, and for the brave people who have shared their stories so that you might not feel so alone.

To Frank, who taught me how to ask the right questions.

To Sarah Bessey, one of my favourite authors, who believes everyone can *play* and do theology to make change.

1
The Discipline of Suffering

What happens when you grow up in a church tradition that sees life and belief in God as simple, factual and straight forward, and then you get plunged into suffering that raises complexities about faith that are not easy to answer?

There is always a choice. We can take the easy way out and stay with simplicity and safety and deny the contradictions of our experience. Or we can do the opposite and walk away from what we believe. The third option is the hardest; it requires grappling with the deep issues and making sense of our situation. That is what this book is about.

I am grateful for my church tradition because it taught me that the most important thing in my life is my relationship with God. This gave me a great foundation for my faith. However, it did not give me a safe place to ask the hard questions that suffering raises. Neither did it equip me with the tools to do this task well. I had to find them on my own. This took work, and the task is by no means complete, as with older age comes more and new issues to face. Life can be cruel and kind. It is unpredictable, hard and often unfair. And yet a life built on the living Jesus Christ is one where if we are courageous enough to step out into the unknown of the *whys*, we will find he is Emmanuel, God with us.

Perhaps the biggest challenge we face when we try to make sense of our experiences and who God is in the midst of our suffering is the paradox posed by our circumstances. Suffering can make us better people, and it can take us closer to God. But the deep, confusing pain can also take us further away from our faith. So, the challenge of suffering becomes one of finding a way to God through the darkness of our pain. When we step out and do this, at times we will feel like we are going around in circles making no progress, or that we are groping along the ground not seeing clearly where our next step is meant to be. We might think that it would be great if someone would give us a candle, a match, or perhaps a glow-worm – anything to help us see the way forward to a solution. We find it hard to understand when God seems silent and unresponsive, not appearing to answer our requests for assistance.

As a child of postmodernism,[1] I understand the dark loneliness of this process to be one of deconstruction, where we question everything we believe to try and resolve the inconsistencies between our understanding and experience, to find a new meaning that makes sense within both the story of our life and the greater story of who God is. Faith in this context of suffering should not simply react against our experience in anger and disillusionment. It needs to push through our despair and doubt. We need to reach beyond these stumbling blocks and find a way to grow, learn and change despite them.

---

1 Postmodernism is a late 20th-century Western movement that is characterised by scepticism, subjectivism and relativism. It is suspicious of reason and alert to the way ideologies can assert and maintain power in society.

For followers of Jesus, then, the challenge when we are suffering is to match our intellectual understanding of our faith to the way we live and experience life. A gap or contradiction between these two things is not sustainable. It causes cognitive dissonance, not to mention its emotional fallout. So, if how we see and understand God is undermined by our life experience, we need to do some soul searching to reconnect these two things back together. Either how we understand God needs to change, or who we are and what we are doing needs to change. More often than not, the two processes need to happen in unison.

We do not need to be fearful of this process of deconstruction. This is because faith in God challenges the nihilism and apathy of postmodernism by offering us hope and a purposeful way forward out of doubt and despair. It embraces the process of picking our situation apart and spurs us on as we move through reconstruction to the other side, healing and making sense of who we are and who God is. It is about going deeper.

I believe that successfully reconstructing our life in the face of suffering transforms us; we grow in our faith and become more Christlike. The good news of Jesus Christ invites us to persevere in our pain, reconnect to ourselves and God, reconstruct our faith and find hope.

Plenty of people have trodden this path before us and succeeded. Paul says in Romans 5:3–5 that

> *we also glory in our sufferings, because we know that suffering produces perseverance; perseverance, character; and character, hope. And hope does not put us to shame, because God's love has been poured out into our hearts through the Holy Spirit, who has been given to us.*

We find a similar sentiment in James 1:2–4:

Consider it pure joy, my brothers and sisters, whenever you face trials of many kinds, because you know that the testing of your faith produces perseverance. Let perseverance finish its work so that you may be mature and complete, not lacking anything.

Yet this is such a countercultural way of thinking, as our society tells us that we need to feed our happiness and dull our pain any way that we can.

Scripture tells us that pain is an opportunity for growth. It is the challenge to finally grow up and become mature. And this is why suffering is a spiritual discipline.

In Christian mystic tradition, the pathway to God was thought to come through love or suffering. Both ways involve giving up control of our life – either by choice or because everything of value has been forcefully taken from us through our circumstances. Whichever way this happens, we end up rethinking our life and what we are living for. In a postmodern context, it means pulling our story about our life apart and then trying to rewrite it God's way. In the process, we find a new knowledge and understanding that brings hope and freedom amidst the struggle.

If life was a jigsaw puzzle, it would be true to say that many of us spend our time constructing our life on our own, carefully working to place each piece, with the hope of creating a whole picture at the end. The fault in this approach is that it is *we* who are placing the pieces, and the picture that we thought we were going to end up with might not be the best outcome for our life. When our life is deconstructed through suffering, the puzzle is smashed. We lose sight of the picture we are making, and we have to start placing the pieces all over again. This time, the challenge is to place the pieces with the help of Christ, working to God's agenda for the finished design and not ours.

I share this metaphor of the jigsaw puzzle as a way of illustrating why the path of suffering is one of the main pathways to God.[2] The key lesson is letting God dictate the direction and terms. Counter to what society tells us, we find redemption of our pain through embracing it and trusting God with it and despite it, rather than in seeking escape from it. This process requires endurance and perseverance. The discipline of suffering is not a process that can be rushed. Patience is required.

My own journey with suffering – and, as it turns out, the pathway to developing a strong faith – started when I was 14 years old. At the time, I struggled with acute back and nerve pain because one of the vertebrae in my back had slipped out by seventy-five per cent. I should have been enjoying my life in north-west Tasmania as a carefree adolescent, self-absorbed, doing the things I liked. Instead, my life was derailed. I was used to getting the highest mark in most of my classes at school, but my health problems caused me to miss months of school because basic tasks like sitting in a classroom became impossible. I had two spinal fusions, and my education became completely disrupted. This was further compounded by my parents' decision to move to Melbourne, which removed me from my extended family and friends.

My back pain forced me into solitude, as did our move to Melbourne. I started to discover that God was my place of refuge and provider of strength. Looking back, I now see that my suffering allowed God to lay a firm foundation for my faith – a faith that was real and lived out daily.

---

2   Rohr, *The Naked Now*, p. 122.

I gradually recovered, although I expected my disability would catch up with me later in life and lived with a fear that the severe pain would return. This happened at the age of 27, when I was pregnant with my son. I struggled just to walk. Since this time my pain has been fairly constant, and my disability continues to worsen with age. It has caused me to make some hard choices, including to only have one child and take positions at work that are sustainable with regards to my health.

Now in my 40s, the pain has become a normal part of my life. It keeps me honest, and it means I rely on God for everything. It has forced me to let go of any illusions I am in control. I've had to completely overhaul the way I live. The limited energy that I have is carefully channelled into the few things that really matter and which I feel God has called me to. Through this hard road, God has changed my character and shown me his faithfulness and compassion. I still get afraid of what the future might bring, but I am continuing to learn that my help comes from him (Ps 121).

Through my experience of suffering, I have discovered that I am not alone. And you are not alone either. Jesus Christ is our brother in suffering. In his death on the cross, he entered into all our pain and journeyed with us in it. The good news of the resurrection is the hope that our suffering can be redeemed both now and eternally. The discipline of suffering is a partnership between us and God to start the process of redeeming our pain, and that of the world around us. This does not mean stopping the pain. It is a creative process of bringing transformation, new life and hope to the present and the future.

STORIES, LANGUAGE AND MEANING

To inspire and comfort you, I will share the stories of other people who have courageously made this journey and come through the darkness with their lives and faith reimagined.

God invites you to take a similar journey together with him, so that he can co-author your story and give you hope and light in a dark place. This book will provide you with some tools for this journey – tools that help you move from feeling shattered, deconstructed and stuck to a place where you can start to dream again.

One of the most useful tools is the humble story, redeployed to help us explore our own thoughts. People think in *words* and *pictures*. Emotional pain and problems can lead to unhealthy thinking, which damages and disfigures us in all sorts of ways – seen and unseen. Such thinking can leave us in a vacuum where we have no words at all to describe or express our experience and make sense of it. This is one reason why we benefit from going to see a pastor, therapist, friend or family member when we have a problem. Talking it through helps us to take a group of disjointed ideas and memories and place them into a meaningful narrative. Prayer can serve this same purpose, because whether out loud or within our head, we are speaking to God using our thoughts.

This is important, because words, language and stories provide us with our identity. When we place our experiences into a sequential order, we form our autobiographical memory – our unique life story. When we process an individual event down to the last detail, we reframe the impact that this has on our life, our understanding and how we see the world. These stories do not have to be based on our own experience. Our lives can be shaped by the stories and experiences of other people, through conversations, books, media, songs and the Bible.

It is possible to study these words, language and stories in a more formal manner using specific, knowledge-based tools, or processes. These can help us to get to the bottom of how we formed our beliefs about our life and who we are, and how we understand our faith and who God is. We will focus on two of these processes:

- descriptive contextualising
- functional contextualising.

These processes sound more daunting than they are. When put into practice, they can help open up whole new ways of thinking and allow God to have the space to speak into our lives.

Descriptive contextualising

The process of descriptive contextualising[3] helps us study our words and actions in context, leading to greater understanding. It is used in a variety of disciplines – including philosophy, sociology, anthropology, literature and biblical studies. The common thread is the search for meaning through story, language and words.

In this book we will look at three approaches to descriptive contextualising:

- social constructionism[4]
- narrative therapy[5]
- hermeneutics.[6]

---

3 Contextualism describes a philosophical view that emphasises the context in which a word or action occurs. Words can mean different things depending on the situation in which they are used. So, 'knowledge' and 'truth' depend on the context in which these words are used.

4 Social constructionism highlights the importance of culture and context in understanding and gaining knowledge about the society we live in, and how we see ourselves within it.

5 Narrative therapy is concerned with how our personal stories shape our lives and how we see ourselves.

6 Hermeneutics is the study of biblical (and other) texts. It includes exegesis, which is a critical explanation and interpretation of Scripture that tries to discover the original meaning of a passage through understanding the literary and cultural context in which it was written.

All three emphasise the importance of examining meaning – either within our society, within ourselves, or within a piece of literature (e.g. a biblical text). They pick apart how our culture informs our identity, what our internal narrative says about ourselves, and how our understanding of the word of God contributes to our thoughts and beliefs.

They are all language tools that help us to probe our knowledge of the world and bring in light to help us see where our dreams for our life and self-narrative might have gone wrong, and how we move forward into a healthy faith and life.

Functional contextualism

Functional contextualism focuses on a detailed analysis of an individual person's thinking patterns. With origins in behavioural psychology and science, it is another postmodern deconstruction tool that helps us address the individual thoughts that subtly shape and direct our actions. These idiosyncratic smaller stories play in our heads throughout the day – as words, phrases, pictures and memories – telling us very specific things about ourselves and who we are. Their presence is so familiar that we often do not even notice them. Collectively, these thoughts can be a problem. Placed alongside the good news of Christ, we are invited to allow God's Spirit to change these patterns of thinking and renew our minds so that we are no longer trapped in our pain.

In this book, I invite you to go on a journey of exploration to look at your own stories of suffering and deconstruct any unhelpful knowledge and understandings that you have been holding onto. In doing so, you will be able to re-evaluate the dreams you have for your life and your narrative about yourself and God, and transform those subtle but powerful thought stories that come into your mind. We will do this through examining

- our *myths*, which can get us stuck in a painful place and distort our idea of God
- our *dreams*, which can be shattered but then re-dreamed in light of the good news
- our *narratives*, which can get us stuck in a problem but can be re-storied with hope
- our *stories*, which can be identified, renewed and rewritten with the help of the Spirit.

It is my prayer that through this journey, you will gain a greater understanding of yourself and God, and that you will find hope and courage to walk a new path and change your mind. Be encouraged that God promises to walk with you in your pain as Emmanuel, God with us. God feels what we feel and promises a future where all things will be redeemed and made new.

> *Praise be to the God and Father of our Lord Jesus Christ, the Father of compassion and the God of all comfort, who comforts us in all our troubles, so that we can comfort those in any trouble with the comfort we ourselves receive from God. For just as we share abundantly in the sufferings of Christ, so also our comfort abounds through Christ (2 Cor 1:3–5).*

SECTION 1
Myths

2
Christian Myths We Believe about Suffering

My brother used to run marathons and liked bushwalking and rock climbing. He lived in Germany, working his dream job as a biomedical engineer designing medical equipment. Then one November he got severe chest pains and went to the hospital. After running some tests, the doctors gave him the terrible news that he had Stage 4 lung cancer. It was a complete shock to us all that someone who had never smoked in their life could be diagnosed with such a thing. It was especially hard on our family because he was living in Europe at the time, and we were separated geographically and limited in how much we could support him.

He lived for another 18 months, but the situation was made more difficult because throughout his illness, he believed that God would heal him and he would not die. He could not reconcile his faith with his experience of life. For a very long time it did not allow him to accept that suffering was a part of life, or that God might not rescue him from the pain that confronted him.

Three weeks before he died, he went for a check-up and the oncologist told him that they would not let him return home. He might only have four weeks to live, and he needed to be admitted to hospital for palliative care. Right then and there he was faced with his own mortality and the harsh reality that he was not going to be healed. I am thankful that at this point he began to feel a great sense of peace. His whole attitude changed, and he was able to say goodbye to people and plan for his death.

His firm belief that God would heal him had prevented him from returning home to Australia. We flew my mother over to be with him, and at 4pm each day I used to call him on the phone to talk. Even so, it was a difficult time for all of us. We remain thankful for the precious people from my brother's church who took turns sitting with him 24 hours a day in the hospital and the beautiful family who looked after my mother during the last three weeks of his life. I am grateful that I was the last person he spoke to and got an opportunity to say goodbye, even though this had to happen over the phone.

This painful personal experience got me wondering about why we are so intent on believing that God needs to rescue us from great suffering. Holding a belief that God will heal us if we have enough faith is not an uncommon thing for Christians to think, and it's a mystery why God heals some people and not others. But to believe in healing to the exclusion of seeing the possibility of a path of suffering can be quite unhealthy.

I miss my brother still and wish that he was part of my life. He died at the age of 41. So, I am conscious that even though he was older than me, I have already outlived him. I also recognise the impact of his faith and witness to the people around him in those last three weeks of his life. The service held after his death was a powerful opportunity to share the message of Christ with the people he worked with and the community he lived in. It reminded many of us not to take our own life for granted and to live it well. It inspired some people to return to their faith and re-join a faith community. Good came out of a terrible situation.

Unfortunately, there was also a lot of pain. When something tragic happens, it often brings out the best and worst in people. They can say the most hurtful and discouraging things. The words sting because there is usually some truth in them, and they tend to be insensitively mistimed. For example, telling me my brother had 'gone to glory' a couple of days after he died a scary death of suffocation did not land well in my ears. Other things that people said quite frankly took me to an even darker place, and for a time I believed that it would have been better that I died rather than my brother.

While time will ultimately heal the pain of the clumsy words that other people say, what does not always leave us is the faulty thoughts that linger afterwards. If our theology of God and suffering is poor and inadequate, we will not move forward. I liken these thoughts to myths because they are like half-truths. For example, there is truth in the statement that God could heal my brother, but this did not happen. It is also true to say he had gone to be with God when he died, but the way he died was terrible and I was left in grief. These myths can be quite harmful and discouraging, and rather than making sense of our situation they usually undermine our view of God and how we see ourselves. Myths can be very destructive because they take us away from faith and our trust in God. I believe we need to confront these myths and stare them down to reclaim the faith and life that God wants for us.

At this point it would be helpful to challenge some of the common my ths that people face during difficult times in their life and grapple with them to see why they are so toxic.

TACKLING THE CHRISTIAN MYTHS WE HOLD ABOUT SUFFERING

'All things work together for good ...'

I have often joked about implementing a tax where I take money for every time a Christian friend or counselling client complains to me that in the midst of their emotional pain someone quoted Romans 8:28: 'we know that in all things God works for the good of those who love him, who have been called according to his purpose.' Their general response is that they feel crushed and worse than they did before the person offered them this nugget of advice. Maybe you have felt the same way.

The advice is unhelpful because what people really need while they are metaphorically sitting in ashes and scraping their sores with pieces of broken pottery (Job 2:8) is someone to be there with them, mourning alongside them. In psychological terms we would call this 'validating their pain'. This means we do not pronounce judgement, offer advice or try to fix the problem for them. Instead, we patiently and intentionally choose to sit with them in their pain and feel it with them. This is one of the main lessons in the book of Job. We are to stop and just *be* with a person in their suffering, and not be like his wife who famously said, 'Curse God and die!' (Job 2:9) or his friends Eliphaz, Bildad and Zophar, who after sitting with him in his pain for a while, concluded he must have done something wrong to bring this much suffering upon himself.

We tend to say platitudes like Romans 8:28 as a universal bandaid. So why do we say it? I wonder if it has more to do with making the person who offers advice feel like they have contributed something so that they can move on and stop thinking about and feeling the pain of the other person. Yet it has the reverse impact on the person who is suffering because it actually amplifies the story of pain in their head and makes it more unbearable. Hearing someone say that pain is for our good can take us to a place of despair. We ask ourselves, how can this possibly be good? And we intuitively know it is *not* good. It is therefore not surprising that when quoted out of context, this verse can cause the suffering person to question the goodness of God.

We are reminded that if we love our fellow Christians, we will not do something that will cause them to stumble (1 John 2:10). Rather, we are to 'Rejoice with those who rejoice; mourn with those who mourn' (Rom 12:15). Let's not be so frightened to take the time to share our sadness.

At this point you might be still wondering about Romans 8:28. When it's not taken out of context and is instead understood within the wider setting of chapter 8, we see that Paul is trying to encourage us in our sufferings as they 'are not worth comparing with the glory that will be revealed in us' (Rom 8:18). He says, 'the Spirit helps us in our weakness. We do not know what we ought to pray for, but the Spirit himself intercedes for us through wordless groans' (Rom 8:26). For 'in all these things we are more than conquerors through him who loved us' (Rom 8:37), and nothing 'will be able to separate us from the love of God' (Rom 8:38).

I do think that suffering can work for our good, as it brings us closer to Christ and forces us to depend upon him. It refocuses our life. And I believe that this is the direction that Paul is trying to lead us in Romans 8:28. I wonder what Paul would say about our quoting him out of context? He would probably tell us to please stop. And he might have something to say about his thorn in the flesh and how God told him 'My grace is sufficient for you, for My strength is made perfect in weakness. Therefore most gladly I will rather boast in my infirmities, that the power of Christ may rest upon me' (2 Cor 12:9).

'You must have done something to deserve this'

Next up is the victim blame game, where we say or imply a person must have done something to bring the situation upon themselves. We leap to the conclusion that they deserve what is happening; sometimes we might go so far as suggest they sinned. Whether we use the word 'sin' or not, the implication of this statement is that the problem is caused by the individual person and is their responsibly. If only life was that simple. Not everything that happens to us is within our control, neither are we always to blame.

The unrecognised pain of this statement is that victims have often come to this conclusion already, and in their misery, despair and doubt, they feel defective and unfixable. It is therefore extremely unhelpful for their friends, family or even complete strangers to come up to them and explicitly state this when they are already well and truly thinking it.

At this point I need to acknowledge that sometimes we do cause our own disasters, and we can deserve the consequences of our actions. For example, if we drive while drunk, we are culpable if we have an accident. If we are unfaithful to our partner, then they might leave us. We need to own these things. But these things aside, what do we do with the belief that we somehow deserve to suffer because we have done something wrong?

In asking this question, we are forced to grapple with our understanding of the character of God and how God sees us. Consider

Exodus 34:6–7. In verse 6, God is described as compassionate, gracious, slow to anger, forgiving, and abounding in steadfast love and faithfulness. It goes on to say that God 'does not leave the guilty unpunished; he punishes the children and their children for the sin of their parents to the third and fourth generation.' What do we make of this? How do we reconcile these two verses? This statement does not necessarily mean that our suffering is due to the sin of our parents, our own sin, or that our mistakes will be passed down to our children. When we read this passage in context, we see God is giving Moses the Ten Commandments and forming a covenant with humanity. God's desire is to have relationship with us. He is not concerned about whether we have made mistakes; rather, his judgement is aimed at people who reject him and do not follow his ways.[1]

This line of thinking is expanded further in Ezekiel 18:20–21, where it says, 'The child will not share the guilt of the parent, nor will the parent share the guilt of the child. The righteousness of the righteous will be credited to them, and the wickedness of the wicked will be charged against them.' We are all judged according to whether we love God and live a life of righteousness in relationship.

Jesus himself made it clear that the sin of our parents did not determine our own level of suffering and sickness (John 9). After coming across a man who had been blind from birth, the disciples asked Jesus, 'Rabbi, who sinned, this man or his parents, that he was born blind?' (9:2). Jesus replied that neither was true, 'but this happened so that the works of God might be displayed in him' (9:3). He then healed the man, which drew the attention of the Pharisees

---

1   BibleProject. 'Does God Curse Generations?', BibleProject Podcast, ep. 5, 14 September 2020, https://bibleproject.com/podcast/does-god-curse-generations/

who completely missed the significance of the healing and instead decided that Jesus was a sinner for healing someone on the Sabbath (9:4–16). As for the man, they dismissed him as one 'steeped in sin at birth' and therefore did not listen to him (9:34). Jesus later told the man he had healed that he came into the world 'so that the blind will see and those who see will become blind' (9:39). Jesus, in effect, challenged this whole idea of the connection between physical disease and sin. He chose instead to draw attention to how God can work miracles in what seems like a hopeless situation.

Of course, a contemporary understanding of blindness from birth means that we assume there is a biological reason for why the man was born this way, and it is unlikely that he or his parents caused this to happen. Sometimes people become sick through no fault of their own; it is just part of living in an imperfect world. My own back problem is one example of a situation like this, because it was caused by a developmental issue. My parents did not cause it. It was just part of living in an imperfect world where genes mutate and things go wrong. I would say that like the blind man, this disability has certainly been so 'the works of God might be displayed' in me (John 9:3), as the pain and struggle has caused me to focus on God and not rely on my own strength to do things.

We know from the accumulation of research in health and mental health that many physical and psychological illnesses and even our temperament are partly genetic.[2] However, it is our interaction with the environment around us that determines which genes get switched on, and our families are part of that environment. This is

---

2   Kaplan & Sadock, *Synopsis of Psychiatry.*

why our personal strengths and weaknesses, and even how physically healthy we are, have a lot to do with our family.

If one of our parents struggled with an addiction, there is a chance we might have one too. But an addiction is not due to genes alone. It will require a mix of genes, plus an environment where we either saw addiction as a coping method or as a way of avoiding pain, combined with us intentionally exposing ourselves to something potentially addictive. This is why it is not inevitable that we will get an addiction just because our parent has one. Life can take us down a different path where we learn another way to live, make healthy choices, confront our problems and use effective coping strategies.

What I am really trying to argue is that saying someone must have in some way caused their own suffering can be ignorant and naive. Few of us know a person well enough to be able to judge them, and Jesus warns us against trying to take the speck our of our brother's eye when we have a log in our own (Matt 7:3–5). And in response to Job's friends who believed Job must have done something very bad for God to be punishing him with so much suffering, God let them know how angry he was with them because they did not speak the truth about him (Job 42:7).

Perhaps there is one further aspect to this argument that is often neglected but still important. That is, that sin is not a purely individualistic issue. Many types of suffering are due to societal-level problems like social change, stressful work conditions, gender discrimination, social exclusion and human rights violations.[3] These problems, which individual people have very little control over, can also contribute to distress and poor mental and physical

---

3   World Health Organisation, 'Mental Health'.

health. We need to acknowledge that such problems are our collective responsibility and stop victim blaming.

'God gives and takes away'

There is a popular Christian song[4] that includes the lyrics 'He gives and takes away', meaning that God gives us good things, and then he can take them away as he chooses. Many people I know struggle with these lyrics because they cannot come to terms with the type of God that this statement is inferring. Why would a good God give us things and then take them away only to cause us pain? This is a good question, and we need to address it because it has implications for our understanding of God's nature. If we believe that God actively gives and takes away things in our life, then it can feel like God is unfeeling, fickle and untrustworthy.

The idea that God gives and takes away comes from the book of Job, where it says in 1:21 that, 'Naked I came from my mother's womb, and naked shall I depart. The LORD gave and the LORD has taken away; may the name of the LORD be praised.' At the beginning of this chapter we are told that Job was a man who feared God and lived a life that was blameless (1:1). God says to Satan,

> 'Have you considered my servant Job? There is no one on earth like him; he is blameless and upright, a man who fears God and shuns evil.'

> 'Does Job fear God for nothing?' Satan replied. 'Have you not put a hedge around him and his household and everything he has? You have blessed the work of his hands, so that his flocks and herds are spread throughout the land. But now stretch out your hand and strike everything he has, and he will surely curse you to your face.'

---

4   Matt Redman and Beth Redman, 'Blessed Be Your Name', *Where Angels Fear to Tread*, Worship Together, 2002.

The LORD said to Satan, 'Very well, then, everything he has is in your
power, but on the man himself do not lay a finger.'

Then Satan went out from the presence of the LORD (Job 1:8–12).

Thereafter Job loses his family and all that he owns, and this is why
he says what he does in Job 1:21.

The reason this passage causes so much angst is that it has particular implications for how we view the sovereignty of God. Andrew
Wilson,[5] pastor, historian and theologian, argues that God was an
active participant in Job's affliction through the actions of Satan. He
then adds that our comfort in such situations comes from knowing
God is in control. However, I find this argument difficult to swallow
because it takes a narrow, literal view of the book of Job, which is
part of the rich wisdom literature of the Old Testament. Wilson's
argument fails to take into account what we know about God from
the whole of Scripture, and it presents us with a conflicted God that
seeks our good but is active in bringing adversity.

It is interesting to note that Wilson was writing in direct response
to a series of blog posts by New Testament scholar Ben Witherington,
who experienced grief from the sudden loss of his 32-year-old
daughter from a pulmonary embolism. Witherington writes, 'God
did not do this to my baby. God is not the author of evil. God does
not terminate sweet children's lives with pulmonary embolisms.
Pulmonary embolisms are a result of human fallenness and the
bent nature of this world.'[6]

He goes on to say that he does not believe these things are
predestined by God because God is merciful and compassionate,

---

5   Wilson, 'Does God Give and Take Away?'
6   Witherington, 'Good Grief'.

full of light and love, and the idea that God gives and takes away is bad theology. His reading of Job emphasises that it was Satan and not God who took away everything from Job. God allowed this to happen, and when we take in the whole narrative of this book, we see that God's will for Job's life was for good and not harm. I have to say that my reading of Job is closer to that of Ben's. There is a great difference between allowing things to happen and intentionally making things happen.

We also need to weigh up Job 1:21 with our understanding of God based on the whole of Scripture. For example, in the book of James we read, 'When tempted, no one should say, "God is tempting me." For God cannot be tempted by evil, nor does he tempt anyone' (Jas 1:13).

And the Jesus I meet in the New Testament in the Sermon on the Mount says,

> *Which of you, if your son asks for bread, will give him a stone? Or if he asks for a fish, will give him a snake? If you, then, though you are evil, know how to give good gifts to your children, how much more will your Father in heaven give good gifts to those who ask him! (Matt 7:9–11).*

God is portrayed here as Abba Father (Matt 6:9) – a parent who wants to give us good things when we ask for them, meets our physical and material needs (Matt 6:25–34), comforts us (Matt 5:4) and shows mercy (Matt 5:7). Jesus is presented as Emmanuel, God with us (Matt 1:23). God is not in the business of creating harm for us. God is like a good and perfect father.

The core problem here is that if we overemphasise the sovereignty of God, we become stuck because our idea of God is inadequate and distorted. God is much more than powerful, wise and in control of the universe. He is a God of love, and this has important relevance to our experience of pain.

'Light shines through broken jars of clay'

Another statement popular in contemporary Christian thinking is that God uses broken clay jars because the cracks allow God's light to shine through more brightly.[7] If you look on the internet and social media, there are memes, sermons and blogs about this topic. So why is this not a helpful thing to believe?

In 2 Corinthians 4, Paul, in the context of sharing the gospel, writes about how God shines in our hearts, and that we have this treasure in clay jars 'to show that this all-surpassing power is from God and not from us' (2 Cor 4:7). He then goes on to talk about suffering. The bookends to this conversation are the statements that 'we do not lose heart' (2 Cor 4:1, 4:16). This is a great image of how God uses ordinary clay vessels, or we might say, an ordinary plastic container from our kitchen cupboard, as messengers of the gospel. The whole point is that people are drawn to the light of the gospel and not to us. We are just ordinary.

It is important to note that nowhere in this passage does it talk about the clay jars being cracked or broken. In fact, I would wonder at why you would store anything in a broken pot (or broken plastic container), so this idea really does not fit the metaphor that Paul is using.

If we explore this logic a little further, a cracked pot (not a crackpot) implies that we as people are broken and that God uses us in our brokenness. There is some sense to this, as Paul says God's

---

7 Dykes, D. 'God Uses Cracked Pots', 11 August 2010, https://www.sermoncentral. com/sermons/god-uses-cracked-pots-david-dykes-sermon-on-parable-widow-149216?page=5&wc=800; Meyer, J. 'Light Shines through Cracked Pots', Online Prayer Partners [Facebook post], 10 May 2013, https://www.facebook.com/OnlinePrayerPartners/posts/light-shines-through-cracked-pots-by-joyce-meyer-let-not-those-who-wait-and-hope/359458650820433/

power is made perfect in his weakness (2 Cor 12:9) and that he can face the challenges in his life because God gives him strength (Phil 4:13). I do not, however, concede that God working in our weakness equates to us being broken.

The reason why I find this difficult to reconcile is that I don't believe God wants us to be broken. Broken people, especially if this is either psychological, emotional or spiritual, are more like leaking vessels that ooze out pain and affliction rather than God's grace and light. In our brokenness we tend to lash out at other people around us, project our problems onto them, and unconsciously hurt them because of our own misery. And we can be blind to these destructive patterns. We tend to see God as if it was through a broken pane of glass. Our sight is distorted, so the image of God that we see is disfigured by our own pain and suffering.

Jesus came to provide healing and transformation to us and the world around us. To meet God through Jesus therefore necessitates that we undergo a process of change. We become a new creation and the old self passes away – something that is only possible through Christ (2 Cor 5:17). The good news of Jesus Christ can certainly be stored in ordinary jars so that it is not us, but the light within us that people are drawn to. The glory is given to God. To hold this treasure, we need to be whole and unbroken, or on the journey to healing. When I think of the people that have had the most impact on me in my life, it is those who speak from a place of healed brokenness who have shaped me the most. The story they tell is one that glorifies God and speaks of how God restored them and made them whole.

Likewise, we need to remember that Christ did not stay crucified. He rose again on the third day and was both divine and human, bearing the *healed* scars of his death but heralding a new kingdom of life that does not end.

STORIES AND NARRATIVES MATTER

These *myths* about suffering are important, because even if we are not consciously aware of them, they influence the way we cope with and respond to adversity, and how we see God. Many people get theologically stuck or feel such a depth of hurt from what is flippantly said to them amidst their pain that they turn away from God, or are so discouraged that they leave the church. For others, these myths will be the very thing that prevents them from following Christ.

I believe these stories have power because they contain a bit of truth that has been twisted just a little so that it distorts either the way we see ourselves or God. If there was no truth in them, we would find it easier to dismiss them from our thinking. Jesus warns us that the devil is the 'father of lies' (John 8:44). He does not speak the truth. Lies are his native language. And the worst and most harmful lies are the ones that contain a fragment of truth warped just enough to cause the maximum damage to us. A helpful analogy can be found in the experience of psychological abuse. The perpetrator often chooses to state something that has some truth in it but twists it in some way. The words penetrate the mind of the victim, who, over time, is worn down with this rhetoric until they believe it and are defeated by it. Our thoughts can work the same way. This is how my own response to the hurtful words of others took me down the path of thinking it would have been better if I had died and not my brother.

But Jesus is 'the way, the truth and the life' (John 14:6). I find this description and contrast helpful, because it identifies that lies do not come from God. God is in the business of shining a light on untruths and evil. We are going to join in with God's work over the following chapters by exploring the problems in our own story and faith, in order to cut through these lies and distorted thoughts and find hope amidst our pain.

The power of this book lies in challenging how you think about your own suffering, and reading about the testimony of other people who have lived both with and through their own. I invite you to read some of the experiences people shared with me about the hurtful things that were said to them during the worst of their pain. I have recorded them here so that you do not have to feel so alone in your own experience and have the courage to explore the destructive and painful words and stories that have arisen in your own mind.

BROOKE: ABANDONMENT IN MARRIAGE

I kept going to church. People would ask me where my husband was, and I would say 'we've separated', then they would ask 'what happened?' They wanted all the grizzly details, no doubt so they could use them as fodder for gossip. I missed out on social invitations because we were no longer a couple. I became isolated. I felt guilty because I thought marriage separation should not happen to a Christian. My sister-in-law was disgusted and held a judgemental Christian view about my situation.

JAMES: PARENT OF CHILD WITH A SEVERE DISABILITY

People would say 'It's not as bad as it could be' or 'Well, at least he's not a vegetable', but I could separate myself from that person and see that they were uncomfortable and did not mean it. Sometimes people's remarks would minimise the severity of our situation or try to point out the silver lining. I recognise the temptation we often have to end a conversation with a positive, and this is why people say these things.

JOSHUA: YOUTH STRUGGLING WITH FAITH

We were talking about creation, and most of the group accepted a literal interpretation of Genesis where the world was created in seven days. I asked what if there were other ways of interpreting chapters 1 and 2 because I thought it strange for faith and science to be in conflict. They would open their Bibles and quote Scripture to denounce my ideas. I did not feel safe in that environment because they were not willing to listen and condemned me for not accepting what the leaders believed. I wanted an opportunity to discuss things openly without criticism so I could grow in my faith.

KARLY: MINISTRY LOSS

After 32 years of service with a Christian organisation, I was forced to resign. People I thought were supportive of me shunned me. One person has apologised since and told me they were warned not to speak to me. I never told people the reason why I left unless they specifically asked. Sympathy was given, but the anger I felt was never acknowledged. They were stunned and did not respond. It would have been better if they had recognised how terrible my situation was.

KIM: HAVING A SAME SEX-ATTRACTED CHILD

I avoided conversations about same-sex attraction because it is a sensitive topic and the last thing I needed was for someone to say something unhelpful. We needed to love and accept our daughter, protect our family and fix our relationship with her because it took her so long to tell us. We only told people we thought were safe. One person said, 'She's studying at university, so of course she's going to be influenced by these ideas.' Another said, 'It's just a stage she is going through.' I wish I had not said anything and tended to shut off after that, and thought *Why did I say something?* People would also share the example of Jesus talking to the woman at the well in the Gospel of John as a way to 'love the sinner but hate the sin', thinking that would help. But this is not what this passage is really trying to say. People twist Scripture for their own agenda.

MICHAEL: MINISTRY BURNOUT

During the burnout phase, tears kept flowing and I couldn't get them to stop. A person saw me crying and mocked me for not being able to stop. The leadership at my church knew I was burning out and were supportive. The people that were causing conflict said, 'I had lost contact with God's Spirit.' This was more to justify their perspective. At the time I knew they were wrong.

PHOEBE: PARENTING A CHILD WITH A SERIOUS MENTAL ILLNESS

I was sitting with my Christian friends, sharing, and a friend was describing her child and how well they were going with their relationships and school. Then I shared my struggles with my daughter, and someone said, 'Isn't that so interesting that one person has a daughter who is so well behaved and the other is not.' I cried right there in front of them all, but no-one offered me any compassion. This comparison was hurtful and made me feel small, like a bad mother. What is worse is that it happened in what was supposed to be a safe space with caring Christians, so it took a long time to move past.

RICHARD: DEATH OF A GRANDCHILD

People recounted suffering in their own life, but it sounded like less than how I felt. Their words only added to the pain – like lemon in the wound instead of ointment. They aggravated my suffering, and I reacted by changing the topic and did not share anymore.

These experiences people shared with me give us insight into just how much malformed theology, judgement and insensitivity can be found within the church. The common experience when confronted by these words is for people to withdraw and feel more isolated in their suffering. I believe that we as the church need to be more compassionate and less judgemental and follow the example of Jesus who brought love, acceptance and healing to other people in their pain. The core of the good news of Christ is that God knows our hurt and despair and feels it with us; he died for us, and he gives us the resurrection hope for a new future where one day creation will be renewed and the pain will be gone.

ENGAGING IN THE DISCIPLINE OF SUFFERING: CONFRONTING OUR MYTHS

Exercise 1. Identify the myths spoken to you and surrender the painful words

- What discouraging things have people said to you at times of pain in your life? What impact did these words have?
- Are there some beliefs about suffering that you have absorbed from other Christians that have caused you to stumble?
- Why did these things have such a huge impact on you? How have they shaped the way you see God?
- Write down the painful words on a piece of paper.
- Commit these thoughts and feelings to God in prayer.
- Decide to let go of the pain that was caused by these words and ask for grace to do this.
- Do this symbolically by destroying your piece of paper.
- Pray through the problem with another person.

Exercise 2. Forgive the speaker or teacher of the words

Jesus teaches some hard things about forgiveness. He says,

> For if you forgive other people when they sin against you, your heavenly Father will also forgive you. But if you do not forgive others their sins, your Father will not forgive your sins' (Matt 6:14–15).

And again,

> So watch yourselves. If your brother or sister sins against you, rebuke them; and if they repent, forgive them. Even if they sin against you seven times in a day and seven times come back to you saying 'I repent,' you must forgive them (Luke 17:3–4).

When we read these words, it is easy to consider them rather idealistic. We are baffled about how to put them into practice, and to be honest, sometimes we either do not want to forgive, or the pain we feel makes the task seem all but impossible.

Research actually supports what Jesus teaches us. We need to forgive, because in carrying around all the hurt and stress we are damaging ourselves. A metaphor to describe this is like holding onto hot coals, or swallowing poison and hoping the other person dies.[8] Holding onto hurt only serves to hurt us. Studies have shown that forgiving other people lowers our blood pressure, heart rate, muscle tension, stress and distress.[9] It has significant health benefits for us.

Not only this, but you might have noticed that in not forgiving, our anger and resentment creeps out of the cracks in how we relate to other people. It comes out in the form of bitterness, rage, anger, brawling, slander and malice (Eph 4:31), and I would add to this list gossip, resentment and jealousy. You might recognise symptoms in your sarcastic comments, snide remarks or cold heartedness to another person.

Yet we are challenged to 'Be kind and compassionate to one another, forgiving each other, just as in Christ God forgave you' (Eph 4:32). The key point is that we have been forgiven, and this is why we need for forgive other people.

Positive Psychology, which is an approach to psychology that has criticised the overemphasis on mental illness and instead advocates for focusing on wellbeing,[10] offers a useful process we

---

8   Harris, *The Reality Slap*, pp. 162–163.
9   McMinn, *The Science of Virtue*, pp. 47–49.
10   Ibid., pp. 62–63.

can follow to help us forgive other people.[11] It involves a number
of steps:

- *Telling the truth.* We need to take the time to open up and tell
  someone what happened. This could be a friend, mentor,
  family member or counsellor. It needs to be someone we
  trust, and we need to discuss the problem in detail.
- *Acknowledging anger.* We need to acknowledge the depth
  of pain that we feel, which might include anger, hate and
  resentment.
- *Being concerned for the other.* We need to get to the point where
  we can see the person who offended us as a person God loves.
- *Recognising, remembering, repenting.* We need to recognise that
  we all have the capacity to hurt other people. Even if we did
  not have power to control or stop what happened to us, we
  can hurt others.
- *Making a commitment to change.* We need to look forward and
  change both ourselves and the community around us. This
  might mean being an agent of change to bring justice and
  healing to both ourselves and other people.
- *Holding onto hope for the future.* We can strive for reconciliation.
  Even if it is not possible with the person who hurt us, we can
  work towards meeting the deep need for it in our community.

This model is very helpful because it gives us a map to follow in
our search for healing. It places our pain within the context of our
wider community, and it challenges us in how we live and respond
to other people. The hardest part is letting go of our pain, because
the reality for many of us is that we cannot be reconciled to the

---

11   See ibid., ch. 2.

people who hurt us. Sometimes this is because we do not have the power to hold them accountable for their actions, or they are not sorry, or they might not be aware of the hurt they caused us. This leaves us in a difficult situation where we need to learn to accept that we will not be able to achieve a perfect outcome.

SECTION 2
Dreams

3
Cultural Dreaming

The Great Australian Dream is to own a suburban house with a backyard for our kids to play in, have a free education, find a job we enjoy, and possibly get married and have children. What we do not realise, however, is that this particular narrative of life is culturally value laden. That is, it is informed by a set of implicit values that underpin the cultural preferences of our society. As people who live within Australia we are influenced by this dream, even if we do not buy into all aspects of it. We, and other people, often judge our success and happiness based on how closely we live up to this standard. This can make our sense of satisfaction precarious. And over time, it is getting harder to attain. For many of us, at some point, the dream will either be unattainable or shatter.

If this basic template of expectation was not enough, my generation (Gen X) was also fed the story that a successful professional woman could have a full-time career and a family and do both of these roles well, simultaneously. Even to the point where I remember being in a mentoring meeting for female academics at my university and being told that breast feeding and changing nappies during a business meeting is completely okay, and that is how you hold down a full-time leadership position while starting a family. You are expected to be like a superwoman.

I can then add another layer to cultural expectations when I think through what my faith tradition implicitly taught: that the ideal Christian life was one of full-time service, where you sacrifice everything for the gospel. Both ministers and missionaries were held up on pedestals, as if they were somehow superior to normal Christians as they had perfected living out the faith in a way that the average person could never do.

Combined, these are weighty expectations to live up to. When I put them in writing, they even seem absurd now. But when I reflect back on the personal dream that I had when I was in my twenties, I did buy into most of this cultural propaganda. I expected that I would get married, have kids, buy a house, have a job, live out my faith and find my sense of belonging in my family. I wanted to serve God with all of my life, wherever that took me and no matter what I needed to sacrifice to do this.

I have since wised up to the realisation that you cannot do all these things well. It is impossible to do so, because some of these dreams assume and depend on a life that is controllable, where we are the masters of our own destiny. But the reality that confronts most of us is a life which does not conform to our dreams and where our control is limited. Our plans can get derailed by health problems, fractured family relationships and problems at work.

The recent COVID-19 crisis has helped expose the problems created by some of the dreams we have for our lives. Despite our advances in technology, we did not have a vaccine for this deadly virus instantly available for our use. For a time, it posed a threat to our health and wellbeing, plunging our country and the world into uncertainty. Everything we held onto as part of our identity was threatened, including our finances, employment, education, health, connection to friends and family, and our way of life.

Many people struggled to cope with this situation because they felt they had no control over their circumstances. This was particularly the case during lockdowns, when the threat to our health was at its worst and where our movements and choices were most curtailed by government regulations. There was tangible concern and fear about contracting the virus. In Melbourne, we were put under curfew and had our lives severely restricted for weeks on end. We were separated from our family and friends, and we were isolated from workplaces, educational institutions and other social support structures. There was a collective sense of helplessness. Life became very small.

The impact of this societal-level experience of suffering was that many people faced financial problems, lost their jobs and became disconnected from friends and family. We were unable to make hospital visits, or be with our loved ones as they passed. We experienced higher rates of mental illness, domestic violence and suicide, and we could not celebrate weddings, births, graduations and other important milestones. We were faced with the reality that our Australian Dream was not guaranteed and might not be attainable. Many people felt their dreams for their lives were threatened or shattered.

The reality of life is that we do not need a pandemic to derail our dreams. We have limited control over many things in our lives. If I look back to my mid-30s, I had most things I wanted. I was married, had a son, a professional job. I had travelled, served in ministry, and I had close friends and family. Then, in the space of a couple of years, my brother died of cancer, my son was severely bullied at school, my marriage broke down, my health was shattered, and my financial security was no longer guaranteed.

My life became deconstructed to the point that it was all in tiny pieces on the floor around me. When we find ourselves at this point, we often do not have the tools or scaffolding to put the pieces back together again to create a whole that is meaningful and fulfilling. As a result, we land in a very dark place that is often lonely and filled with despair. It is not surprising, then, that at some point in our lives, many of us will become disappointed and disillusioned with life and God. All because our circumstances are preventing us from living this story, the Australian Dream, and *our dreams* that we believed we could turn into our reality.

WHAT OUR CULTURE TELLS US

Part of the problem is that many of us will actually find that aspects of our cultural ideal are possible because we are in a privileged position compared to much of the rest of the world. We have access to medical treatment when we are sick, and we have a reasonable living standard. Australian statistics show that the top 20 causes of death in our country in 2021 were diseases of the elderly, including heart disease, dementia, stroke and respiratory illness, with a median age of death of 82.0 years, except for suicide which had a median age of death of 45.8 years.[1] Life expectancy has increased from 51.1 years in males in 1891–1900 to 81.2 years in 2018–2020, and for females from 54.8 years in 1891–1900 to 85.3 years in 2018–2020.[2] These statistics show just how fortunate we

---

1   ABS, 'Australia's Leading Causes of Death, 2021'.
2   AIHW, Deaths in Australia.

are, because we generally do not live under the threat of physical disease and death, and we live a relatively long life.

This can lull us into a false sense of security, because in our privileged position we are relatively free to pursue happiness. We live with little awareness of our own mortality, and we are usually not exposed to extreme poverty, disease, religious persecution or political unrest. This means that when things go wrong, we react to adversity as if it is not the norm. Problems like cancer, chronic illness, mental illness, disability, job loss, the death of a child, childlessness, abuse or relationship breakdown are not part of the life we envisioned for ourselves. They can catch us off guard.

Leigh Sales, Australian journalist and author, writes about how her dreams were shattered after the traumatic birth of her second child, where both their lives were at risk. This experience made her question her self-sufficiency and control over her life.[3] She lost her sense of security in the world and sense of self. This even made her ask some hard questions about how we come to terms with unexpected tragedy, how we can keep going and how we can live. We realise we are just as vulnerable as the next person, and that tragedy can strike us all.

What in effect happened to her is that the dream or ideal for her life, which was constructed by our culture and society, felt broken. Her happiness was shattered, and she did not know how to put it back together again. This can happen to us as well. These times in life can be devastating, but they also provide us with a unique opportunity to see past our dreams and go deeper into exploring what is really important to us.

---

3 Sales, *Any Ordinary Day*, p. 11.

CULTURAL BLINDNESS

It is unfortunate that sometimes we can become so comfortable with the story our culture is selling us that we are blind to how it creeps into the way we express our faith. We can unwittingly lull ourselves into a false sense of security, believing that God will protect us from disaster and pain. I know that I have caught myself thinking along these lines. As an example, I thought that going to work cross-culturally with a mission agency meant that God would spare me from certain kinds of suffering. I know that I am not the only person to fall for this trap, as while I was living in Central Asia, two of the people I was working with had a car accident. They drove on black ice and could not brake in time to avoid a collision. The car was written off, and fortunately they were not injured. At the time, the question everyone seemed to ask was, why did God allow this to happen to them? What was implied but not spoken was that they thought missionaries should be under God's special protection. I wonder if this thinking is flawed? God loves all people equally. A good God would not want harm to come to anyone. We are not special because we sign up for ministry. We are exposed to just as many problems and risks in an imperfect world as the next person.

Solomon made a helpful observation that 'All share a common destiny – the righteous and the wicked, the good and the bad' (Eccl 9:2). Life does not treat us differently because we live good lives or believe in God.

The same message is echoed in Jesus' teaching. In no way does he tell us that his followers will be saved from suffering. In Matthew 5:43–48, he says that we need to love our friends and our enemies, and be perfect in this way just as God the Father is perfect, for 'He causes his sun to rise on the evil and the good, and sends rain on the righteous and on the unrighteous' (Matt 5:45). What I take this to mean is that God's love is not more focused on Christians just because of their faith. God loves all people, and in this way treats us all equally. 'For God so loved the world [not just Christians] that he gave his one and only Son ...' (John 3:16). We are called to the same Way, to love all people and not discriminate. We live in an imperfect world where bad things happen, and not everything is in our control.

Many of us struggle to get our minds around the concept that God does not intervenc in the world to stop suffering. Natural disasters and illness happen, and they are part of the world we live in, a world governed by natural laws. People are not perfect, and they harm each other in many ways – through genuine mistakes; through their own faults and weaknesses (intolerance, ignorance and unresolved hurt); and intentionally because of hate, anger, malice, resentment and jealousy. They do this as individuals, families, social groups and as nations. Because God gave us free will, he does not necessarily intervene to stop us.[4]

Romans 8:20–22 describes the situation this way:

For the creation was subjected to frustration, not by its own choice, but by the will of the one who subjected it, in hope that the creation itself will be liberated from its bondage to decay and brought into the freedom and glory of the children of God.

We know that the whole creation has been groaning as in the pains of childbirth right up to the present time.

This passage does not mean that God set things up so that we would suffer. It means that the world was created with the hope

---

4 I acknowledge here that prayer does make a difference.

that all humanity would come to God of its own free will in love. God's hope for us is that our dreams are redeemed.

Even though crises happen occasionally in our lives, most of our awareness of suffering and pain will not necessarily come through devastating and stressful life events. They will instead be an accumulation of many day-to-day issues that build up to make our life hard. Small problems that defy the dream we are told is attainable. I like how Michael Spence, ordained Anglican minister and Vice-Chancellor of the University of Sydney, describes it in his interview with Leigh Sales about the death of his wife, Beth, from cancer:

A lot of the time, life is just hard, and even for people who have a relatively benign life, a lot of the time, stuff's just hard. And it's okay to say stuff's hard, it doesn't do anyone dishonour. It's alright. It's just giving people space to be human.[5]

His statement provides a helpful insight, causing us to consider whether the dream our culture sells us is realistic or helpful. If we hold to it too tightly, we will become bitter, resentful, disillusioned or disappointed, or alternatively trapped by the need to succeed and realise our unrealistic dreams.

THE DREAM IS BROKEN

Many of us have realised that being financially and materially wealthy, or searching for happiness by fulfilling our desires, does not lead to a life that has meaning or satisfies our deepest human needs. It is like chasing after the wind (Eccl 1:14). King Solomon discovered this truth in ancient times. Ruler of Israel from 970 BC

---

5 Sales, *Any Ordinary Day*, p. 46.

to 931 BC, he has been rated as the one of the richest people in world history. The Old Testament tells us that while he ruled, his nation was prosperous and peaceful, and his wisdom was known through the surrounding nations (1 Kgs 4).

Solomon had the view that self-indulgence, where we buy whatever we see and like, is futile (Eccl 2). Such self-indulgence can have serious consequences. In Proverbs 5, Solomon explains that sex outside of a long-term, committed relationship can corrupt our character and lead us away from the path of life (Prov 5).

Yet, despite his wisdom, Solomon accumulated 700 'wives of noble birth' and 300 concubines, who ultimately were his downfall (1 Kgs 11:3). They gradually turned his heart away from God, and he turned to worshipping the gods of the nations around him, taking on their traditions and practices in the process (1 Kgs 11).

Solomon's life became a cautionary tale, an example of the damage that can be wrought in our lives when we believe the lies our culture sells to us – that sex will make us happy, that power is a worthwhile pursuit. Power can move us away from even needing a faith because we believe the lie that we can live on our own and don't need God. We become our own god in our selfishness. Life is about us, and getting what we want.

1 John 2:15–17 warns us:

> *Do not love the world or anything in the world. If anyone loves the world, love for the Father is not in them. For everything in the world – the lust of the flesh, the lust of the eyes, and the pride of life – comes not from the Father but from the world. The world and its desires pass away, but whoever does the will of God lives forever.*

Living for ourselves and accumulating wealth does not work. Our affluence does not protect us from adversity. It does not make us happy. In fact, a constant state of happiness is not something we can realistically achieve.

Our culture has become increasingly individualistic, and our social and intimate relationships are more fractured as a result. This has left many of us feeling unsupported and alone. We compare ourselves to other people on social media and feel envious of the lives they seem to lead, feeling that our own life is inadequate and unfulfilling. There is a real gap between what we consider to be our ideal life and how we are actually living.

Far from making us happy, our material possessions and our need for status and position have made us slaves to our standard of living. We feel controlled and restricted by our jobs, mortgages and the weight of financial debt. To our surprise, the very things that we thought would make us happy actually work against our happiness and trap us.

Our private despair is partly reflected in the statistic that in Australia 43.7% of people will experience some form of mental illness over their lifetime.[6] As many as 21.4% (or 4,198,700) people aged between 16 and 85 years had a mental disorder in a 12-month period.[7] While many of us will not die prematurely of a physical illness, the suicide rate is high, making it into the top 15 causes of death in our country, in 2021.[8]

Johann Hari, UK journalist and author of *Lost Connections*, argues that our existential crisis, and its accompanying high rates of depression and anxiety, is due to a disconnection from meaningful work, other people, our values, the natural world and a hopeful

---

6   ABS (2022), 'National Study of Mental Health and Wellbeing'.
7   Ibid.
8   ABS (2021), 'Australia's Leading Causes of Death'.

future.[9] It comes from trying to avoid the pain of our past traumas and feeling disempowered. This leads to a sense of hopelessness and a numb repetitive engagement with the routine of life.

Apathy is one likely result. Elie Wiesel wrote, 'the opposite of life is not death, it's indifference.'[10] This concept holds a great truth, because we are seeing in our culture a form of suffering that is taking our humanity away from us. It comes in the form of nihilism and apathy. It leaves us paralysed. Such disillusionment about life does not discriminate. It can impact any age group.

THE CHALLENGE OF ADOLESCENCE

Adolescence (12–18 years) is meant to be a period of maturation and transition between childhood and adulthood. One of the main challenges we face during this time is to work out what we are going to live for. We need to find purpose and a reason to get up each morning. This inevitably requires going on a search for meaning, and working out what kind of person we want to be. It is the process of re-evaluating the values and beliefs we have inherited from our parents and the ones pushed upon us by our culture and society, and deciding whether to embrace or reject them.

We can try living for ourselves and turn to sexual relationships, substance use and superficial fulfillment so we feel good in the short term. Alternatively, we can choose the path of doing nothing and not working out our purpose, but if we do this we usually end up apathetic, directionless and devoid of a belief system that can anchor us during difficult periods. Both options lead to a dead end

---

9   Hari, *Lost Connections*.
10   Wiesel, 'US News and World Report', p. 249.

because they are self-focused – they seek to satisfy our own desires and our thinking is centred on ourselves.

The best outcome is found in facing the challenges in front of us one at a time. In doing so, we gain purpose and clarity about our future and who we want to be; we are able to accept ourselves, and have a sense of belonging and place in our community; and we learn to be resilient and persevere through difficulties. We find fulfillment when these things come to us through our relationship with God and other people.

Our success or failure in navigating this developmental period and successfully forming an identity will have repercussions for our future. If problems are left unresolved, they will come back to haunt us later in life – as will our tendency towards using destructive coping strategies. But history also tells us that the energy, idealism and fearlessness of youth has the power to change the world and create a bright future for individuals and communities when it has a solid value base and is rooted in God.

THE QUARTER-LIFE CRISIS

The quarter-life crisis is something many young adults are coming up against in their mid-20s.[11] It is characterised by a general dissatisfaction with life, where we wonder if everyone else has a better life than us. This feeling is spurred on by social media and the deception that the ideal lives that other people portray are actually real, when in fact they are just a filtered public persona. We wonder why our life is not as together as the lives of other people around us. We become fearful about making decisions in case

---

11 Jones, *Is this it?*

they are wrong. Full independence and *adulting* look scary because we are afraid to take risks in case we fail.

Key questions that we ask ourselves at this time centre on the purpose of life and how to make important decisions. We can become paralysed by having too many choices, and we do not want to take the risk to follow through and commit to one. Decision paralysis impacts our work, where we live, our relationships and how we spend our time. As we are more geographically mobile, we are more prone to rootlessness and the feeling that we do not have a community in which we belong. We may get trapped in thinking that things were better when we were younger and avoid thinking about the future. We may work for the wrong reasons and hate our jobs. We may become easily dissatisfied with our employment and unsettled at the increasing casualisation of the workforce. We get lonely, struggle with being single and have an unrealistic idea of romantic relationships that sets us up for disappointment.

There is a need at this time to wrestle with how God fits into this struggle, with the outcome informing our motivation and direction in the choices we need to make. First and foremost, it is not important how the world sees us on social media. It is how we stand before God that should direct every choice we make. We need to be countercultural and belong and contribute to a faith community so that we feel connected to other people and realise that we work not to please ourselves but to honour God in all we do. Our relationships need to be based on godly love and be gracious, characterised by the fruits of the Spirit (Gal 5:22–23) rather than focused on what we can gain from them. We need to have faith and trust God with our future, and step out and take risks when we need to.

THE CHALLENGE OF MIDLIFE

Midlife (age 35–55 years) presents another challenge. We often joke about the stereotype of men having affairs or women having plastic surgery and going on fad diets. But it can be anything but funny for both the individuals and their families who are struggling through it.

Key issues that both men and women struggle with at this time are the loss of their physical youthfulness, feeling trapped in their job and/or struggling with the weight of responsiblity to care for their family. We can feel God's judgement because of what we are struggling with. We want to have some choice, but we are burdened and therefore feel constrained by our responsibilities. These kinds of situations can lead to depression or attempts to feel good through a short-term fix – like changing our physical appearance or how we dress, or by losing weight or getting fit. We consider ways of opting out of work, retiring early or changing career. We might re-evaluate our priorities when we have children, when they start or finish school, when they leave home, or due to the emptiness of our marriage. We might consider having an affair. This struggle has implications for our faith. Depending on how we resolve the battle with our will, we might let go of our faith in God to follow other gods that we think will meet our selfish needs, or we might reject faith in a god all together.

We need to concede that a conflict of values exists. Our culture measures our worth by our financial, work and material success. But our faith tells us that pursuing these things is like chasing the wind. Faith is not just about making a decision to be a Christian. It is a Way of life that happens moment to moment in the drudgery of the everyday, in the little things we do as part of our daily routine, and in major life events. Indeed, 'God seems to believe that the process of moving through life is as important as the end result.'[12] Our worth is determined by God's gracious love for us and not how the world sees us. Christ invites us to go deeper into our faith with the pain, rather than run after what the world tells us to dream about.

A CRISIS OF WHAT?

The common thread that weaves through all these life transitions is the feeling of being trapped or helpless in our circumstances. To resolve this feeling, we need to address two key issues: finding a meaning, identity and purpose; and surrendering our will and life to God.

Jesus says in John 8:31–32 that 'If you hold to my teaching, you are really my disciples. Then you will know the truth, and the truth will set you free.' He goes on to have a conversation with the Jews about the idea of slavery, pointing out that 'everyone who sins is a slave to sin' (John 8:34). I would like to suggest that the sin we most struggle with in our culture is one of individual self-focus. The thing we desperately need to be saved from is ourselves and our own willfulness.

To live according to God's plan for us means to love him first, love the people around us (Matt 22:37–39) and to seek his kingdom. To live according to the Way of Jesus Christ is to give up our will to God and follow Christ daily, taking up our cross (Matt 16:24–26). Then, Jesus tells us, 'if the Son makes you free, you will be free indeed' (John 8:36).

---

12   Conway, *Men in Midlife Crisis*, p. 132.

As you read the following stories about other people's broken dreams, I want you to reflect on your life and where you feel a pain and disappointment because of the huge gap between your actual life and where you expected to be. These times in life can be devastating, but they also provide us with a unique opportunity to see past our cultural dreams and go deeper into exploring what is really important to us.

BROOKE: ABANDONMENT IN MARRIAGE

I was married at 20 and had a dream for a home and family and to be comfortable; my husband would be the bread-winner and I would stay at home. We had a dream to go on a three-month trip around Australia, and as a family we did everything together. When he left me, I was shattered and felt rejected. Maybe I could have done more, and this would have made a difference? I felt unwanted, with low self-esteem. I had to rebuild my life. I had a choice to blame God and turn back and believe I was a failure or throw myself onto God. I never got an explanation for why my husband left me or an apology even after 32 years of marriage. He filed for divorce, appealed through legal aid, and was dishonest regarding the property settlement. He reneged on child support.

JAMES: PARENT OF A CHILD WITH A SEVERE DISABILITY

My wife and I hoped to have three kids that were normal, with a two-year gap between – two boys and a girl, or two girls and a boy. I had a dream that our oldest son would be able to play with his little brother, but this dream was obliterated after our youngest son was born severely disabled. I wasn't so concerned about the loss I felt as a parent. Myself and my wife have been more impacted by the fatigue of being carers for our son. As a family we have a modest dream of owning a home suitable for our disabled son's needs. This has not happened yet. The gap between our children was not what we expected. Our oldest is now nine years and our disabled son is seven, and we are expecting our third child in the next six months. When I first found out our son was disabled, I doubted that I could love a disabled child even though I have a brother with Down syndrome. At the time I felt devastated, like I had been given a sentence of doom, and started looking at other disabled children with walkers or misshapen heads and found their disability grotesque and very frightening. I was aware that there is shame in society around having a disabled child and felt judged that there was something wrong with me as a man. I doubted God could change my perception from horror to joy.

JOSHUA: YOUTH STRUGGLING WITH FAITH

Faith was a cultural or social thing I needed to participate in rather than being a personal relationship with God. I didn't really know God; I was going along with what people wanted me to do. This eventually wore me down and I stopped trying to develop a genuine faith. My questions were my way to develop faith. I stopped asking questions and became compliant with what was expected, and faith became emotional and not intellectual. It meant that my mood dictated my closeness with God. When leaders upset me, I would feel angry with God or distant, versus worship nights where I would feel overwhelming joy. This was confusing.

KARLY: MINISTRY LOSS

I had thought I would stay in my role until I retired. I had worked there for 32 years. My view was partly to protect the other staff in the organisation. Leaving my job threw everything up in the air and destroyed my dream to care for other people in ministry. It brought a new dream earlier than expected – one of member care for other missionaries. This was meant to be for retirement, but when my daughter reminded me about the dream it gave me reason to stop and reflect.

KIM: HAVING A SAME SEX-ATTRACTED CHILD

I tried not to think what our kids would be like. I was more concerned about what kind of person they would be, if they had a deep peace and relationship with God, were respectful, trusting and relational. I wanted to get along with them. I felt gutted that she hadn't trusted us as parents to tell us. It took her two years to build up the courage to say something. She said that her family was so important and worried it might break if she told us. There was fear about how saying she was same-sex attracted would impact the family and the way we thought about faith issues and teaching on same-sex relationships. She said that she had always felt different.

MICHAEL: MINISTRY BURNOUT

I had a dream that the church would thrive despite appearances. I thought that if I kept plugging away God would provide a breakthrough. But when I became burnt out, I realised that God was not going to rescue the situation. I felt empty.

PHEOBE: PARENTING A CHILD WITH A SERIOUS MENTAL ILLNESS

All we wanted was for our kids to be normal. I feared that they would have a disability. She was born normal but was full-on and did not cope with boundaries. I just wanted her to get through school and not die due to her impulsivity, and not emotionally hurt anyone else too much, including her siblings. I took one year at a time.

I see God's hand in her being kept safe. She moved schools for Year 12, away from her peer group and finished school ok. I see the same mental health symptoms in my mother, and some in myself, and look at other aspects of her behaviour that are similar to my husband's family. I find this is confronting.

RICHARD: DEATH OF GRANDCHILD

I dreamed that my granddaughter would come to know Jesus and express her love for him so people would be impacted for the kingdom. She was intuitive picking up people's feelings. I dreamed of her expressing that in ministry to others. She was not fearful. I could see what she was going to be.

ENGAGING IN THE DISCIPLINE OF SUFFERING: BROKEN DREAMS

Exercise 1: Your dreams

Honestly reflect on whether your dreams are rooted in your culture or your faith? Do you see a tendency in yourself to want to rebel and meet your own needs instead of surrendering to God and his way? Are there parts of your life where you have retained control rather than giving them up to God?

Think about whether you have fallen into the trap of buying into the following cultural values. If you think any of these, or something else, is creating a problem in your life, surrender it to God now.

- living for yourself
- feeling dissatisfied
- avoiding commitment
- chasing experiences and pleasure
- wanting freedom from responsibility
- focusing on sex and superficial relationships
- being money focused
- accumulating unnecessary material possessions
- excessive pride and vanity in your appearance
- seeking power and control
- believing that constant happiness is the ideal.

Exercise 2: Reflect on the values of the Jesus

Jesus taught that the greatest commandment that God gives to us is to 'Love the Lord your God with all your heart and with all your soul and with all your mind' (Matt 22:37) and to 'Love your neighbour as yourself' (Matt 22:39). He also says that,

Whoever wants to be my disciple must deny themselves and take up their cross and follow me. For whoever wants to save their life will lose it, but whoever loses their life for me will find it. What good will it be for someone to gain the whole world, yet forfeit their soul? Or what can anyone give in exchange for their soul? (Matt 16:24–26).

Reflect on what Jesus said and try to measure your life against the values of Jesus. How far short do you fall?

4
Finding God's Dream for Us

In the song 'Dream for You' by Casting Crowns,[1] it talks about how David might have dreamed of being a shepherd, but God had a different plan for him that involved fighting a giant, leading an army and being King of Israel. Likewise, Mary dreamed of marrying Joseph and having a family, but she ended up raising the Son of God. Neither of them grasped the path that God was about to take them on. The point is that we often have a plan or vision for our perfect life, but the idea we have is not always the reality that occurs, and it is not even the best future that we could experience. Faith in God means trusting God entirely and surrendering our will and our expectations for our future, and following Christ in the small and large choices we make. The song invites us to let go and do this.

One of my friends found this song really important when they were going through a tough time in ministry. Their job came to an abrupt end, not through their own choosing. This was both disappointing and out of their control. The song encouraged them to let go of their dream and allow God to lead them to find a new dream.

---

1 Casting Crowns, 'Dream for You', *Thrive*, Sony/ATV Tree Publishing, 2013.

This painful experience led them to start a new ministry which continues to have an impact many people. The song was one vehicle that God used to open their mind to new possibilities and start to think differently. It was a creative means to get them to reflect and gain a new perspective.

A SOCIAL-CONSTRUCTIONIST APPROACH

My friend went through a process of deconstructing their purpose for living and then reconstructing it to find a new reason to work and live. This happened through the challenge of a song. This process is an example of social constructionism – a way of trying to make sense of our shattered dreams. If we utilise it well, it can help us to move forward creatively through our pain.

Social constructionism acknowledges that our social reality is formed by our worldview.[2] Here, 'worldview' refers to the reality held by a group of people. We normally call this our culture, which consists of our values, thoughts and feelings about things that shape the way we see the world. Worldview can be something held by a group of people (e.g. ethnic group) or an individual person.

According to this approach, meaning is socially constructed through encounters between people, and it is dynamic and fluid. Knowledge is influenced by our place in history and our cultural values.

Words and language help form this knowledge because they shape how we see and construct the world. They can also help in the process of deconstruction so that we can critique culture and social practices, and then reconstruct ideas to create change. To aid in this process, social constructivism uses additional ways of presenting

---

2   Galbin, 'An Introduction to Social Constructionism'.

knowledge in the form of story, narrative, poetry, images and other media. It embraces participation and creativity – exactly what we see in the song 'Dream for You', which uses language and music to help us see our faith and our pain in a different way.

CHANGING THE LENSES IN OUR GLASSES

If we are serious about finding a way out of our cultural disillusionment and flawed worldview, we need to identify our current values and place them under a metaphorical microscope so that they can be carefully examined. Although this process of deconstructing our story can be very painful, it gives us incredible freedom to inventively reimagine our life in terms of what is actually important to us, and of course our faith in Christ.

Even more important is to blow the idea of having a right to happiness completely out of the water, because it is not achievable 24/7. Chasing this part of 'the Dream' has only fed our despair and fuelled the pursuit of temporary happiness through material possessions, superficial sexual relationships and the need to succeed.

Recently I revisited Tony Campolo's book *Carpe Diem*,[3] which described the impact the American Dream was having on the North American church. Written more than 20 years ago, it is just as relevant to the North American – and Australian church – today. Campolo argued that in our consumeristic, self-focused culture,

The function of God has been changed. He has a whole new role. No longer is he the object of all worship and adoration. Instead he has become an important means for getting what we now worship and adore – things, or at least the money to buy the things. In our brave new world, we worship the things we have been conditioned to want, and we will be religious if

---

3 Campolo, *Carpe Diem*.

religion can guarantee us the products our democratic capitalistic society turns out by the tons.[4]

According to Campolo, the Jesus that we have constructed is different to the historical Jesus of the Bible. The result is a formulaic version of the gospel – one where we believe that if we do all the things popular Christianity says we need to do, then we will be successful and prosperous. It is commonly referred to as the prosperity gospel. Our faith has become functional, another thing we possess and consume to serve our life. In this context, God becomes a kind of 'super genie' who answers our prayers to address our needs.[5]

Our churches have taken on the surrounding culture, trying to adapt themselves to make faith more appealing to non-Christians. Church is now entertainment, offering a more *seeker*-friendly environment. Mixed with the prosperity gospel, it has resulted in a popularist form of Christianity that is watered down and more palatable to the average person. This form of faith is easy to follow, costs us little and gives us a magic ticket to heaven.[6] But in changing the message, we actually traded off the hard teachings of Jesus about sin and repentance, suffering and redemption, and did not challenge people to go deeper in their faith. We have ended up with a generation of biblically illiterate Christians. So, it is no wonder that when we face huge obstacles in our life, we have no teaching to fall back on. Suddenly faith becomes all too hard or irrelevant to our situation, and we walk away.

The good news about the historical Jesus, found in Scripture, says something very different. Following this Jesus, who is alive and with

---

4 Ibid., p. 46.
5 Ibid., p. 47.
6 Hinn, *God, Greed and the (Prosperity) Gospel*, pp. 157–8.

us today in resurrected form, means that we will pray 'your king-dom come, your will be done, on earth as it is in heaven' (Matt 6:10).

If God's kingdom comes on earth right here and now, that means we are not off the hook. Faith is relevant to how we live our life every moment, and it is not just about going to heaven when we die. We become agents of change. True freedom, the kind that Christ offers to us, comes from willingly giving up material things, our own agenda and individualism. Life becomes about loving God and other people, and placing them at the centre rather than ourselves. All else flows out from this.

I find it encouraging to think about the story of the disciples on the road to Emmaus, walking and talking about the events surround-ing the death of Jesus: 'As they talked and discussed these things with each other, Jesus himself came up and walked along with them; but they were kept from recognising him. He asked them, "What are you discussing together as you walk along?"' (Luke 24:15–17).

Their reaction to this question was that they stood still and looked sad, and then one of them asked him, 'Are you the only one visiting Jerusalem who does not know the things that have happened there in these days?' (Luke 24:18).

Imagine just how devastated they must have been. Everything they had come to think and believe, and what they had invested their life into for the past three years, had just fallen apart. It had all ended in the death of their leader – and the death of their purpose. It is interesting that Jesus responded by patiently going through all of Scripture to explain the things about himself that they did not understand. He was actually reconstructing their story and putting it together into a new understanding and way of seeing Scripture, faith and life.

Despite this detailed explanation, the disciples did not recognise that their companion was Christ until the evening meal, when 'he took bread, gave thanks, broke it and began to give it to them' (Luke 24:30). Then he vanished, and they said, 'Were not our hearts burning within us while he talked with us on the road and opened the Scriptures to us?' (Luke 24:32). When I think about it, this is also often our experience through these times of reconstructing: Christ is with us, walking through the pain as we go, and we hear him through what he says in our hearts and through Scripture, and through the words of other people, gently leading us on to a new way of thinking.

The point of this story is that we do not have to do this alone. There were two disciples travelling the road together that day, and Christ joined them. Likewise, the reconstruction of our story happens both individually and in community. The reimagining of our life after our dream is shattered is only possible through our relationship with Christ and other believers.

If we dare to take this path through our pain, we will find the Spirit leads us in ways we did not think possible.

LIVING BETWEEN WESTERN CULTURE AND JESUS CULTURE

Life as a follower of Christ is complex within our worldview and culture because we have more than one framework through which we see the world. We live between the worldviews of our society and ethnic group, and the Jesus culture.

Adopting a social-constructionist perspective can help us think more deeply about what values underly our society's culture. Table 1 lists some of the overarching values that are part of Western culture, Australian culture and Jesus culture.

In addition to these cultures, each of us as individuals will have our own unique set of values that are usually a combination of the values listed in Table 1 and some that are more specific to who we are. An example can be found in my own experience, which I share at the start of chapter 3.

Table 1: A comparison of the values of Western, Australian and Jesus cultures

Western culture[7]	Australian culture[8]	Jesus culture[9]
Democracy	Freedom and equality	Love of God and neighbour (Matt 22:37–39)
Freedom	Dignity and respect	Surrender of our will (Matt 16:24–26)
Human rights	Democracy	Love (1 Cor 13:4–8)
Rational thinking	Egalitarianism – a 'fair go', so all people can succeed	Faith (1Cor 13:13)
Individualism	Tolerance	Hope (1 Cor 13:13)
Materialism	Cultural diversity	
Progress	Mateship	
Scientific thinking	Happiness	
Capitalism		

These values are important to recognise because they shape our aspirations. In the case of Australia, our emphasis on freedom and equality, and a fair go, have combined with the individualism and

---

7   Broadly speaking, the values held by Western culture come from a 'modern' rather than a postmodern framework. A 'modern' framework values progress, rationality, individualism, the scientific method, and universalism.

8   Department of Immigration and Border Protection, *Life in Australia*.

9   1 Cor 13:4–8.

materialism of Western culture to shape the Australian Dream. These values are not necessarily in harmony with the message of Jesus.

Jesus culture is counterintuitive; within it, the values that are prescribed by society are turned upside down. Consider how Jesus describes the kingdom of God in the Sermon on the Mount (Luke 6:20–26):

> *Blessed are you who are poor,*
> *for yours is the kingdom of God.*
> *Blessed are you who hunger now,*
> *for you will be satisfied.*
> *Blessed are you who weep now,*
> *for you will laugh.*
> *Blessed are you when people hate you,*
> *and when they exclude you and insult you,*
> *and reject your name as evil,*
> *because of the Son of Man.*
>
> *Rejoice in that day and leap for joy, because great is your reward in heaven. For that is how their ancestors treated the prophets.*
>
> *But woe to you who are rich,*
> *for you have already received your comfort.*
> *Woe to you who are well fed now,*
> *for you will go hungry.*
> *Woe to you who laugh now,*
> *for you will mourn and weep.*
> *Woe to you when everyone speaks well of you,*
> *for that is how their ancestors treated the false prophets.*

These teachings warn us against the very things our culture says we should aspire to. It is in turning our back on these things – possessions, food, happiness and popularity – that we live the way of the kingdom.

Jesus builds on this teaching later in the same chapter of Luke's Gospel. He encourages us to love our enemies (6:27); treat people the way we want to be treated (6:31); be merciful (6:36); forgive, rather than judge or criticise people (6:37); give to others (6:38) and bear good fruit (6:45). We are to put his teaching into action, using it as a firm foundation for our life (6:46–49). This is the practicality of what it means to love other people and be part of his kingdom.

EMBARKING ON THE RECONSTRUCTION PROCESS

My encouragement to you is to take the time to really wrestle with the complexity of trying to work out what you are called to live for. There are faults and weaknesses in every culture, just as there are strengths as well. We need to weigh it all up, assessing it in the light of our faith.

Facing a crisis or transition in our life does not need to be a disaster, or cause one. It provides us with an opportunity to re-evaluate what we want to live for and whether we are living consistently with Jesus' teachings, and in doing so, opens up the possibility of a completely different future.

The people who shared their stories in this book have engaged in the hard work of picking up the shattered pieces of their dream and reconstructing it. I have shared their experience again at the end of this chapter so that you are inspired to take the same path.

In the next chapter we explore our faith tradition of lament and how this can be a comfort to us when our dreams get shattered. It shows us a creative way of deconstructing and reconstructing our dreams and faith using poetry, language and metaphor.

BROOKE: ABANDONMENT IN MARRIAGE

I had to rebuild my life. I had a choice to blame God and turn back and believe I was a failure or throw myself onto God. I was blessed by the timing of having grandchildren, and my focus changed to working and earning an income. My family came first, and I could focus on them and other important things, my values and church work. The experience built up my faith and I got involved in prayer ministry. I was open to where God was leading me.

JAMES: PARENT OF A CHILD WITH A SEVERE DISABILITY

My love for my son has grown over time, and this is from God, and an answer to prayer. I enjoy being with him. He sees things differently and has a personality, a sense of humour. He loves his family and still engages in some sibling rivalry with his brother.

JOSHUA: YOUTH STRUGGLING WITH FAITH

I moved to a church where people could have a depth of conversation and were open to challenge so I could develop a more nuanced faith. I wanted a more structured church, so faith was no longer just about emotion and was integrated into my life through discipleship and following the pattern of Jesus and other Christians.

KARLY: MINISTRY LOSS

My daughter reminded my husband and I of another dream we had. It was to provide pastoral care and support for missionaries. I had thought this was for retirement, but the end of my dream – working in ministry in an organisation – brought this other dream earlier.

KIM: HAVING A SAME SEX-ATTRACTED CHILD

I have a new dream that my daughter and her partner's relationship can be common knowledge to our extended family and wider circle of friends, and for my daughter's faith to recover so she can identify as Christian and be in a church community that is accepting. I have found comfort in the way Jesus spent time with outcasts, and think faith is more about how we treat other people than what we say. I now focus a lot more on God's love and grace.

MICHAEL: MINISTRY BURNOUT

I still desire to see the church grow and believe a key value is community. My ministry is now not about location, but about people. I have redefined success as not being about numbers, but more in people's stories interacting with the good news.

PHOEBE: PARENTING A CHILD WITH A SERIOUS MENTAL ILLNESS

My dream for her has now blossomed. Now she is an adult, everyone sees her as a bubbly, creative woman with so much potential and beauty, but there is also a depth of suffering. I hope that at the times when her mental health issues spiral that this does not damage this positivity. She has now taken on the label of having borderline personality disorder and has started to get the help that she needs. My dreams are more positive. God holds on to me and helps me cope. I think bad things happen to good people and have found that contemplative Christians are more able to sit with other people's pain.

RICHARD: DEATH OF A GRANDCHILD

My dream for my family is still the same. I have greater resolve as a grandparent to help my grandchildren come closer to Jesus and realise their dreams, and I treasure them more.

ENGAGING IN THE DISCIPLINE OF SUFFERING: FINDING GOD'S DREAM FOR US

Exercise 1: Define your values and purpose

Remove yourself from your normal daily life and take a couple of hours to be by yourself and pray and reflect on your life.

Our life can be categorised into five main areas: work/education, relationships, hobbies, health and spirituality/faith. Write down what your values are for each area. *Values* are things you believe are important in the way you live. They provide direction, purpose and set your priorities. (They differ from goals because they are not something you achieve.)

For example, if you value having good mental health, you will maintain a healthy work–life balance, sleep 7–9 hours per night, exercise, eat healthy food and take time out to relax.

Work/Education

Relationships

Hobbies

Health

Spirituality/Faith

When you look at your values, is your list consistent with how you live, or is there a disparity? If there is a difference, what is it and why? What changes do you need to make to bring your life more in line with what is important to you?

Think about the values you listed. How do they measure against the life of Jesus? Are they consistent with what you read in the Bible? How might you become more Christlike? What does the Bible tell you about how you should work, manage your finances, and care for your family and health? Review your values in light of these things.

Exercise 2: Consider your character

Character refers to the qualities that you would like to be defined by. What kind of character would you like to demonstrate in your daily living?

Take some time to read through 1 Corinthians 13:4–8.

Love is patient, love is kind. It does not envy, it does not boast, it is not proud. It does not dishonour others, it is not self-seeking, it is not easily angered, it keeps no record of wrongs. Love does not delight in evil but rejoices with the truth. It always protects, always trusts, always hopes, always perseveres. Love never fails.

Which of the characteristics listed do you struggle with exhibiting in your life? Pick one characteristic of love that you would like to improve and actively live out in your life. Try to follow through with practising this over the next week. Ask the Holy Spirit to enable you to make this change.

5
Disorientating and Reorientating Our Life and Faith

Fear can be the most intimidating part of pain. When I was a single parent, life very much became about survival. It felt like I had lost everything, and I still shouldered the responsibility of being a good parent. That, together with my existing chronic pain, left me without a sense of control. Life often felt overwhelming, and God was all I had to cling to.

The problem with fear, though, is that it can blind you and throw you off course. At these times I found it most encouraging to meditate on Psalm 23, and how God was guiding me and walking with me through the darkness when I could not clearly see a future. He invites me to be part of his family and eat at the table with him. God cares about my situation. I do not need to be afraid.

I am not the only person who has found this psalm comforting amidst suffering. Psalm 23, 'The Lord is my shepherd', continues to have an impact in our culture that extends beyond the reach of the institutional church, through music and the arts.[1] It appears in popular songs by artists like Kanye West, Good Charlotte and Pink Floyd, and in films like *Titanic*. Psalm 40, another psalm that is full of comfort when life is grim, appears unchanged and in full in U2's song '40'. While our culture might have a mixed approach to its interpretation of the psalms, the fact that they still appear in contemporary culture demonstrates something about their relevance to what we all struggle with.

Walter Brueggemann, in his books *Praying the Psalms*[2] and the *Spirituality of the Psalms*,[3] argues that the psalms speak to us so personally because they are about the rawness of life. They have been written with passion by people who were at a desperate place in their life, and found themselves in a situation of dislocation. Many take the form of a complaint or supplication. In our reading of these poems and prayers, we discover that the experience of the writer is similar to the one we find ourselves wrestling with, one where our dreams for our life have shattered.[4]

The psalms help us to understand how we are shaped by our own experiences. They take us through movements of language from orientation to disorientation to new orientation. This is similar to the movement from deconstruction to reconstruction, or suffering to redemption. When we move through these experiences, we are engaging in a countercultural activity because our culture aims for order and success and the avoidance of pain and hurt. The psalms, in contrast, articulate the chaos we are going

---

1 Jacobson, 'Through the Pistol Smoke Dimly'.
2 Brueggemann, *Praying the Psalms*.
3 Brueggemann, *Spirituality of the Psalms*.
4 Brueggemann, *Praying the Psalms*, p. 10.

through and show a boldness in taking this directly to God. They cut against culture and dare to complain about loss. They move us from complaint to hope. We revisit this movement time and again, and in the process find that we repeatedly gain our life when we lose it (Mark 8:35).[5]

PSALMS OF ORIENTATION

Psalms of orientation are expressions of life for times when everything is stable and balanced and there are few problems. God is Creator. They speak about creation (Pss 8, 33, 104, 145) and living in a reliable, ordered world (Pss 1, 15, 19, 24, 119, 14, 37) where there is peace and God is faithful (Pss 131, 133). These psalms are a means by which we confirm, individually and collectively, our theology of God. In this sense, they function in a similar way to liturgy – spoken words confirming our unspoken common understanding.

However, just like we need to quote Romans 8:28 ('we know that in all things God works for the good ...') wisely and within an appropriate and empathic context, we need to be careful to use these psalms in the same way. We certainly do not want to misuse them to maintain social control by denying the uncomfortableness of other people's problems and silencing them by over-emphasising blessing.[6]

---

5   Brueggemann, *Spirituality of the Psalms*, p. 15.
6   Ibid., pp. 21–22.

PSALMS THAT MOVE FROM DISORIENTATION TO REORIENTATION

Many of the remaining psalms are not poems and prayers that we will be able to enter into when life is fine and in equilibrium. We visit them when we feel pain, and we find in them what we are already experiencing in our own life. Their words of lament give reality to what we feel, and they articulate it. The evocative language contained in them publicly acknowledges an event or problem in conversation between the writer and God. And in our own experience reading the psalms, we too find a way to express our own situation – our dislocation in our life and our disorientation within it – and share it with God.

In this struggle, there is something powerful about how our complaint to God echoes a kind of death to our dream, because we are acknowledging that it is over. These complaint psalms become a voice for the dying, for pain, for the passing away of something that we loved and held onto.

The great comfort is that these psalms do not leave us in a dark place. They also surprise us, moving us to a new orientation, a new way of seeing things. There is a contrast between despair and hope, chaos and life-giving order. The old is made new. Praise is given to God with thanksgiving, and there is a recognition that God is sovereign. In the words of Brueggemann,

> *The Psalms are an assurance to us that when we pray and worship, we are not expected to censure or deny the deepness of our own human pilgrimage. Rather, we are expected to submit it openly and trustingly so that it can be brought to eloquent and passionate speech addressed to the Holy One.*[7]

---

7 Brueggemann, *Praying the Psalms*, p. 14.

The language of these psalms of disorientation take us from this place of broken dreams and reorientate us to God's position in the larger perspective of life, where he is king, and he is to be praised. Images of destruction and suffering are balanced by ones of a God who governs and provides order, invites us to sit at his table and delights in our celebrations.[8]

We see this movement from orientation to disorientation to reorientation clearly in Psalm 23. It talks about the Lord as our shepherd, then walking through the darkest valley, then eating at a table before our enemies and dwelling in God's house:

The Lord is my shepherd, I lack nothing.
He makes me lie down in green pastures,
he leads me beside quiet waters,
he refreshes my soul.
He guides me along the right paths
for his name's sake.

Even though I walk
through the darkest valley,
I will fear no evil;
for you are with me;
your rod and your staff,
they comfort me.

You prepare a table before me
in the presence of my enemies.
You anoint my head with oil;
my cup overflows.

Surely your goodness and love will follow me
all the days of my life,
and I will dwell in the house of the Lord
for ever.

---

8   Ibid., p. 28.

We are not left hanging in the middle of the darkness. This psalm intertwines our path and God's, reminding us that we are not alone, and we are loved and cared for at all times. The metaphor used, of God as shepherd, is quite evocative and comforting at the same time.

METAPHORS IN THE PSALMS

One of the most powerful literary tools used in the psalms is the metaphor. In the context of this book, we can think of a metaphor as a 'picture story' based on our experiences of everyday life. The psalms use metaphors to express our plight as humans and how we are to understand who God is. They are particularly effective in helping us to explore our pain in a deeply personal way.

The pit

The metaphor of the pit is a common one throughout the psalms. It refers to a place where we are powerless, silent, forgotten and dead. Everything is lost. 'The pit is a place cut off from God so that God may neither help nor be praised there.'[9] As the writer of a psalm does not specify what disaster led to them into the pit, we can easily insert our own experience into the story and join with them in their cry of disorientation. An example is Psalm 40:

> *I waited patiently for the* LORD;
> *he turned to me and heard my cry.*
> *He lifted me out of the slimy pit,*
> *out of the mud and mire;*
> *he set my feet on a rock,*
> *and gave me a firm place to stand.*

---

9   Ibid., p. 33.

He put a new song in my mouth,
a hymn of praise to our God.
Many will see and fear the LORD,
and put their trust in him.

Another word that often appears alongside the idea of the pit is 'Sheol' (Ps 30:3). Contrary to popular understanding, this word does not refer to hell, but rather a place where we are separated from God, without voice or joy or hope. Our faith does not protect us from going to this place; rather, it is the power of God that brings us out of the pit, or Sheol, to a new life, a new dream and a future.

Under the safety of God's wings

Within the psalms we find a powerful counterweight to the metaphor of the pit, one that balances out despair. It draws upon the image of a mother hen protecting her chicks from harm, evoking a sense of warmth, safety and protection. Psalm 17:8 is one example, the writer praying to God, 'hide me in the shadow of your wings.' The psalms provide us with other images with a similar theme – for example, a tent, rock or tower where we can find refuge (Ps 61). When we trust in God to protect us, encouraged and inspired by these images of God's protection, something powerful happens. The power of the pit is broken.

Whoever dwells in the shelter of the Most High,
will rest in the shadow of the Almighty.
I will say of the LORD, 'He is my refuge and my fortress,
my God, in whom I trust.'

Surely he will save you
from the fowler's snare
and from the deadly pestilence.

He will cover you with his feathers,
 and under his wings you will find refuge;
 his faithfulness will be your shield and rampart.
You will not fear the terror of night,
 nor the arrow that flies by day,
nor the pestilence that stalks in the darkness,
 nor the plague that destroys at midday (Ps 91:1–6).

One of the most precious lessons we can learn in life is that we are constantly moving between the pit and the wings. Our lives do not stay static. This is the nature of life. This process of disorientation and reorientation is a framework within which we can understand our experience, and the psalms become a tool to help us articulate it.

VENGEANCE IN THE PSALMS

When we find ourselves in a dark place, a pit, it is human nature to find someone or something to blame for our predicament. A good example is Psalm 35. When we perceive that other people have contributed to our situation, we blame them and wish they had been sent to the pit. We feel a deep need for justice and vengeance for what has happened to us. For many of us, these feelings can be very uncomfortable because they force us to confront the lack of humanity within ourselves.[10]

One of the most uncomfortable aspects of the psalms is what appears to be an unashamed expression of a desire for vengeance (Ps 109). They do not hold back – even if the desire is expressed verbally rather than through action. Brueggemann[11] proposes that this expression of emotion serves a couple of functions.

---

10 Ibid., p. 34.
11 Ibid., p. 68.

First, it is cathartic. It helps us plumb the depths of our feeling with permission, in a way that we would not normally be allowed to do out loud. It legitimises our anger. Second, when we do identify with the words, we find that nothing terrible happens. We are not condemned for it. They are thoughts and words directed at God, not the person who has offended us. It is a way of entrusting our anger to God for him to act upon it.

We must also consider God's response to our cries. Seen in the wider perspective of both the Old and New Testaments, we find that vengeance is not ours; it belongs to God. We do not need to retaliate when someone acts against us. It is not our responsibility. It is an act of faith to let it go and leave it in God's hands. God must then balance our need for justice with his desire for mercy, because in extending compassion to us the other person needs to be considered. It is not God's desire to condemn, but to liberate, and we need to leave room for God to do so. In Brueggemann's words, 'vengeance is the back side of compassion.'[12] God is not indiscriminate with his anger. He is on the side of the faithful, the poor and the needy (Ps 103). On some occasions when God is angry, he chooses not to take this out on the offending persons and directs it inward, taking on our suffering as his own. He chooses to respond with sorrow, rather than justice (Gen 6:5–7; Hos 11:1–9).

The question of how God resolves the issue of vengeance makes sense with the death and resurrection of Christ, where it is addressed once for all. The anger, grief, rage and despair are dealt with in the crucifixion, and we are liberated through the resurrection to new life and the ability to extend compassion to our enemies.

---

12   Ibid., p. 73.

SOLACE IN THE PSALMS

The words of the psalms are one of the few places where we find a full expression of our human experience in all its joy and pain. They explore the depths of human existence and suffering, and we find within them a space for hope.

We will all experience times when, for various reasons, we cannot connect to our faith because of the problems we are struggling with. In these situations, the complaints and acknowledgements of God's faithfulness that are expressed in the psalms meet us in our darkest despair and give us a voice to express our own struggles. We might need to turn to Psalm 40:1–3 to cry out to God, just like U2 did in their song.[13] When things are at their worst, we tend to wonder how long we will have to sing the song of sadness. When will God give us a new song to sing?

The people I interviewed said that waiting in the sadness was one of the toughest experiences they had, because for many types of suffering there is no end. It continues with us through life as a form of open-ended grief and loss. Sometimes I describe it as a strange, peaceful sadness that hangs in the background. It never leaves, but our awareness of it becomes more vivid at specific moments. The psalms were important to these people because they gave voice to the pain, but also encouragement to go on. We need patience not to rush through this experience, as uncomfortable as it is, because God is at work in it. Disorientation has to come before we can be reorientated and the pain redeemed.

In this struggle, God says one thing to us: 'Be still, and know that I am God' (Ps 46:10).

---

13 U2, '40 (How Long)', *War*, Island Records, 1983.

BROOKE: ABANDONMENT IN MARRIAGE

I would read Psalm 4:8 so I could sleep at night, 'In peace I will lie down and sleep, for you alone, LORD, make me dwell in safety.'

JAMES: PARENT OF A CHILD WITH A SEVERE DISABILITY

I would go for walks and pray raw, angry prayers, but they ended with some short confession of God's goodness like the psalms.

KARLY: MINISTRY LOSS

Psalm 121 – I lift up my eyes to the mountains – where does my help come from? My help comes from the Lord, Maker of heaven and earth.

KIM: HAVING A SAME SEX-ATTRACTED CHILD

Some parts of Scripture were hard to read because they weren't that helpful in our situation. It was more useful to hear about the experience of other Christians – through conversation, songs or reading the psalms.

MICHAEL: MINISTRY BURNOUT

I learned to be still. Psalm 46:10 says, 'Be still and know that I am God.'

PHOEBE: PARENTING A CHILD WITH A SERIOUS MENTAL ILLNESS

I related to Psalm 40, because I felt like I was at the bottom of a pit crying out.

RICHARD: DEATH OF A GRANDCHILD

The psalms were most helpful because they are full of feeling, and I was feeling intensely in my grief.

ENGAGING IN THE DISCIPLINE OF SUFFERING: EXPRESS YOUR PAIN

Exercise 1: Read the psalms

Soak yourself in the psalms and explore their depths and breadth. Let them be your voice to God when things are tough. Allow them to take you through the rhythm of disorientation and reorientation, the death of your dream and a hope for a new future.

Explore the metaphors that are used to describe the way God protects and cares for you. Which one do you find most encouraging? Let this metaphor permeate deep into your life and experience, to encourage you in your faith and give you hope.

I recommend that you read one or more of the following:

- Psalm 23
- Psalm 40
- Psalm 46
- Psalm 91
- Psalm 121

Write your own psalm or poem. Express your deepest feelings to God without reserve and see where it takes you. Then sit with these thoughts in God's presence. Pray through what you wrote, and allow God to speak into your experience. End with a time of thanksgiving for the good things you see in your life, and praise God for his faithfulness to you.

Exercise 2: Meditate on Psalm 23

Read Psalm 23 (or another psalm) meditatively either by using a *lectio divina* style or informal method of contemplation. Guidelines for the *lectio divina* method are given below. For the informal method, read the psalm one or more times per day, for an extended period of time. This might be a week or a month. Invite God to speak deeply into your life as you do this.

> The LORD is my shepherd, I lack nothing.
>> He makes me lie down in green pastures,
> he leads me beside quiet waters,
>> he refreshes my soul.
> He guides me along the right paths
>> for his name's sake.
>
> Even though I walk
>> through the darkest valley,
> I will fear no evil;
>> for you are with me;
> your rod and your staff,
>> they comfort me.
>
> You prepare a table before me
>> in the presence of my enemies.
> You anoint my head with oil;
>> my cup overflows.
>
> Surely your goodness and love will follow me
>> all the days of my life,
> and I will dwell in the house of the LORD
>> for ever (Ps 23).

Lectio divina

- *Read Psalm 23.* Read the psalm, listening for a word, phrase, metaphor or part of the passage that stands out to you. Try not to choose this yourself. Instead, let God's Spirit bring it to your awareness.
- *Read and reflect.* Read the psalm again, and think about why the word, phrase or metaphor stood out to you. What drew

you to it? How does it make you feel and think about yourself and God? Pray, and ask God to show you how this applies to your life today.

- *Read and respond in prayer.* Read the psalm again, and pray to God about what you think the Spirit is saying to you. You might like to respond with a quiet prayer of thanks or request.
- *Read, rest and contemplate.* Read the psalm again, and then spend a few minutes in silence before God. You might like to focus on an aspect of God's character. This might be from the passage you just read. Simply sit and immerse yourself in your relationship with God.

Narratives

6
Rewriting Our Narratives

In the Divergent series of books, by Veronica Roth, the main character Tris has to hide the fact that she is different to the other people around her. Her dystopian society is divided into factions, and unusually, she can fit into more than one faction in her dystopian society. This is considered to be 'divergent'. It means that unlike most other people, she is not confined to one way of thinking and therefore cannot be controlled.[1] People like her are considered a threat to the leaders of her society, so they are hunted down and contained.

To add to the constant threat of being found out that she is different, a string of other painful events occur. There is an uprising, and she witnesses her mother die; she is forced to kill her friend Will in self-defence to survive; her dad is killed; and she is betrayed by her brother. It is not surprising that amidst all this grief, she forms a belief in her head that she is the problem, and she is to blame for all the suffering she has witnessed. She cannot forgive or accept herself.

---

1 Roth, *Divergent*, p. 442.

I wonder if this is the place where we often find ourselves when we suffer. The story of our life becomes a narrative of suffering that causes such great pain that we just want to push it away. We can even start to think like Tris and believe that we are to blame, or that we are the cause of the pain. We cannot find peace. We wake up at night after bad dreams. We no longer trust other people or ourselves. Hope is lost.

Thankfully, Tris' story does not stop there. She learns that she was not the scourge of her society but actually the intended solution. Her flexible mind was the gift needed to restore society and help other people.[2] This was the plan that was put in place when the system under which they lived was formed.

This new narrative opened the door for her to start the process of self-forgiveness. She realised that her mother's death was unpreventable. Her mother's heart had always been to protect and save her daughter from harm, and she died doing this. Another friend forgave her for killing Will, and she moved closer to being able to forgive herself. She no longer saw the suffering as her fault. It just happened. Later she went on to find enough love to willingly give up her life to save her brother's, despite his betrayal.

On the final page of the last book in the series, we read this poignant observation: 'Since I was young, I have always known this: Life damages us, every one. We can't escape that damage. But now, I am also learning this: We can be mended. We mend each other.'[3]

Tris' story, although fictional, states some truths that are really helpful. For example, it shows just how painful and destructive a problem-saturated view of our life can be. Here I am referring to

---

2 Roth, *Insurgent*, p. 524.
3 Roth, *Allegiant*, p. 526.

seeing your life in such a way that a problem encompasses your whole perspective on your situation to the exclusion of everything else. Tris' experience shows us that this does not have to be the case. There is great power in transforming a problem-saturated narrative as it can change the way we live.

It was in reading the Divergent series that I found the words to articulate and identify where my own thought pattern was wrong in explaining my suffering. I could see part of my own story mirrored back to me through the character of Tris, and I realised that many of the problems that had arisen in my family were largely out of my control. They were not caused by me or because of me. I just happened to be the person caught up in the mess. The damage caused by life cannot be escaped. In finding this new perspective, I found the freedom and hope to create a new story, just like Tris had done. We all have the opportunity to be mended.

The use of story and how it shapes our understanding of our lives has been harnessed by narrative therapy. This is a method of facilitating change by helping people find a way out of their problem-saturated situation, a new meaning in life, and a way forward to a new purpose and a future worth living for. In other words, we can use this method to unstick ourselves from believing we are trapped in our problems with no hope of change.

NARRATIVE THERAPY

Narrative therapy was developed by Michael White, an Australian social worker who developed an interest in the problem-saturated narratives of his clients. He began exploring ways to help them move beyond their problems and explore new stories and new solutions, and in doing so, find hope. White did this by using tools such as externalising, re-remembering and re-authoring conversations, which I will explain in more detail later in this chapter.

White's therapy is based on developing an awareness that power and culture influence how we think about our place in the world, and that we can be authors who rewrite our understanding of our situation to find new meaning in our suffering, regain hope and have the power to change our future. We do not necessarily need to be the problem.

The text analogy

White's work uses the analogy of text to explain how people make sense of their lives – that is, how they ascribe meaning to their experience through 'storying' it. People arrange events in time so that they can understand and describe themselves, and the world around them,[4] forming a self-narrative. This provides them with continuity and meaning, which they can use to order their daily life, interpret their experiences and understand their identity.

One problem with our self-narrative is that we tend to leave out details and end up with a dominant story that selectively contains the rich detail of life.[5] Over time, as this process continues, much of our actual lived experience (the details that aren't central) remains un-storied and is not expressed. We overlook some aspects of our life story in preference to remembering others. We then live out of and through our dominant narrative, which is like a summary explanation of who we are. This influences the way we interact with and organise the world around us.

---

4   White & Epston, *Narrative Means to Therapeutic Ends*, p. 10.
5   Ibid., p. 11.

Our narrative also evolves over time. Every time we are asked to provide an account of our life, or parts of it, we speak about what happened to us (i.e. we perform the story), just as an actor recites and delivers their lines in a play. Each time we give our account it is slightly different, and this slowly changes our narrative. Or, as White and Epston explain, 'Every telling or retelling of a story, through its performance, is a new telling that encapsulates, and expands upon the previous telling.'[6]

Problems arise when our dominant story is imposed on us by other people or does not allow enough room for our lived experience. We get stuck in our understanding. In order to move forward, we need to identify and generate new alternative stories. These often come from the un-storied part of our life, the details we neglected, and through them we can find new meaning and new possibilities that are not so destructively confining.[7]

For example, as Christians, we can get trapped in the dominant story that we are sinful and always fail at the thing we struggle with the most. The dominant narrative emphasises our sinfulness and how far we fall short of what we want to be like. If we stay in this place, we are vulnerable to focusing on our faults and are probably not going to see beyond them. We are therefore more likely to repeat them. When you think about it, this is a distortion of what the good news is about, because Jesus did not just die, he also rose again. The power of our faith is found in the resurrection. In Paul's words, 'if anyone is in Christ, there is a new creation: everything old has passed away; see, everything has become new!' (2 Cor 5:17). We are no longer under the law of sin and death (Rom 8:12). We

6   Ibid., p. 13.
7   Ibid., p. 15.

live by the Spirit. With this story of renewal, I wonder how differently we might live if we believe we are forgiven, redeemed and loved by God.

KNOWLEDGE AND POWER

We would be naive to think that we as individuals have absolute power over our narratives, as they are not formed within a vacuum, but in relation to the lives of other people around us. We live within social groups and cultures. Even if we do not realise it, there is pressure to be normal, and this is imposed on us implicitly like a form of social control.

It is important to consider, then, how the ideas that underpin our stories are formed and what purpose they serve. While culturally there might be an expectation for us to conform to what the people of our social group do, keeping the *status quo* and being *normal* might not be the best way. For example, accumulating material possessions and wealth is associated with financial security, but Jesus warns us that we cannot serve both God and money (Matt 6:24). Achieving financial security might mean that we need to work long hours and devalue our relationships and faith. This means that cultural normality is not always consistent with being a follower of Christ.

If we're being honest, many of us struggle with the question of how much money we need to live. It is one of the real-life conundrums we face when trying to make sense of what normal is, how our life should be, and the truth about our situation. Another challenge is social control – that is, the power our culture can have over us to pressure us to conform to what everyone else is doing.

We feel conspicuous if we do not comply with what is expected.[8] It has the capacity to impact every area of our life, from the type of car we drive, what we wear and our holiday destinations to how many children we have and who we spend time with.

This social control also extends to how we see people. Our Western society tends to objectify people and their bodies. It divides and categorises us. Our bodies become a thing. We are things.[9] And when our humanity has been reduced to a commodity or object, it is much easier for people in power to exert control through the technique of *normalising judgement*.[10] A great illustration of this is when people don't like something we have done and say that it's *un-Australian*. We are socially shamed to force us to conform. Or thinking from a Christian perspective, we can be told we do not have enough faith. In both cases we are not judged according to our actual worth as a human being, but rather by a set of cultural standards. This devalues and undermines our humanity.

Separating ourselves from our problems can force us to challenge cultural practices and regain our humanity. So, the process of challenging the dominant narrative is essentially political because it questions the controlling cultural narrative and ideology that is imposed on us.[11]

If we think about how this might apply to followers of Christ, consider the way we behave and speak about our problems. We try to comply with what we believe is expected in a particular Christian environment. We put on a moral facade, frantically hoping that

---

8 Ibid., p. 24.
9 Ibid., p. 66.
10 Ibid., p. 70.
11 Ibid., p. 29.

no-one will see through it to find out what we are really like. We talk about everything having a season, using language that comes across as quite strange to anyone outside the church. We actually think that we have to pretend we do not have problems. Our marriage is fine, we do not suffer from depression, we are amazing at managing our money and giving generously, our children are perfect. If only! We can trap ourselves by our own *truth* by thinking that we need to act a certain way to be a Christian. It is a form of social control.

I am not sure if this is how Christ wants us to be. True freedom means living by the Spirit rather than under the weight of Christian expectation or that of our culture. Jesus cautioned us that we need to be careful not to become obsessed with our outside appearance and behaviour. Remember what he said to the Pharisees: 'you ... clean the outside of the cup and the dish, but inside you are full of greed and wickedness. You foolish people! Did not the one who made the outside make the inside also?' (Luke 11:39–40). What is important is what is happening *in our mind and heart*. For, 'the mouth speaks what the heart is full of' (Matt 12:34) and 'What goes into someone's mouth does not defile them, but what comes out of their mouth, that is what defiles them' (Matt 15:11).

If I were to reflect on this problem a little deeper, I think I would question the adequacy of an idea of faith and Christianity that focuses on living good lives, where God will protect us and make us prosperous if we fulfil certain conditions and rules. This way of thinking can tie us in knots. The danger is that if we face suffering, our whole belief system is at risk of shattering because the pressure to comply to the norm implies that we have not done enough, our faith is inadequate, or God is not who we thought. The other problem with this approach is that it tends to create a church of outwardly and superficially religious people who are desperately trying to hide the crippling hidden shame of their imperfect lives.

EXTERNALISING THE PROBLEM

To move beyond being stuck in our problem-saturated story, we need to consider how the problem impacts our life and relationships with other people and God. This process is called *externalising*. It helps us separate from our story and explore alternatives – aspects of ourselves that have been neglected and not expressed. This approach 'encourages persons to objectify and, at times, to personify the problems that they experience as oppressive.'[12]

Externalising helps us to see where our lives are being constructed and constrained by the dominant cultural truth and knowledge. Many times, these problems are rooted in a failure to meet certain expectations and unstated norms. It can be those imposed on us by other people or ones we set for ourselves. Through the process of externalising, we get a different perspective on the problem and our lives, which is potentially very liberating.[13]

In a practical sense, the problem becomes a separate entity that exists outside of us and our relationships with other people and God. This frees us up to get a different perspective:

- We stop blaming people, or God, for our problem.
- We no longer see ourselves as a failure because of it.
- We can cooperate with other people to find ways to escape it.
- We find new possibilities and ways to live that are not dominated by it.

---

12   Ibid., p. 38.
13   Ibid., p. 30.

- The seriousness and weight of our situation is eased.
- We open ourselves up to a new dialogue, no longer stuck within a set narrative.[14]

In essence, we are no longer the problem; the problem is the problem. Externalising our unwelcome situation helps us to see our relationship to the problem and take responsibility for the part we play in maintaining it.

Therapists often use this approach in counselling, referring to *the* eating disorder, *the* cancer, *the* anxiety. When I think of my own suffering, this concept is helpful because I can separate myself from my physical disability and see it as a separate entity. This way it does not dominate my life or my thinking. It is present in my life, but it does not determine how I live or define who I am. Instead, my identity is firmly rooted in Christ.

RE-AUTHORING AND RE-REMEMBERING

An underlying assumption of this narrative approach is that we seek help to resolve painful issues in our life when the dominant story does not line up with our lived experience. Our experience contradicts our story. To reconcile the discrepancy, we need to separate ourselves from our dominant story, and re-remember and re-author the neglected parts of our lived experience. These are parts of our story that happened, but we might have forgotten them, or not processed them deeply, or not noticed their significance and potential for providing a new path forward.

When we re-author our story, we become aware that the problem we are dealing with can only successfully continue if particular

---

14   Ibid., pp. 39–40.

events and people are in place. Once we understand this, we can engage in some emotional and psychological guerilla warfare to sabotage the maintenance of the problem. We begin to see the pattern that maintains the problem, then we start to think outside of it and recognise times when these events and people have not been in place and new outcomes were possible. Next, we can explore questions of what happens when we 'refuse to perform to the requirements of the problem.'[15]

Problems are dependent on their effects to survive. So, disrupting this relationship between the problem and its effects creates change, allowing us to identify ways we can resist the effects of the problem and its demands.[16]

We only need to identify one unique outcome to open up a new way forward. A new narrative can be performed, or spoken, to create new meaning.[17] This approach is particularly effective when it comes to family problems, because it only requires one person to change, to create a cascade of other changes in how people relate to each other, to disrupt the maintenance of a conflict or unhealthy relational pattern. Only one person needs to engage in the performance of a new story and choose not to cooperate with the problem to undermine the problem.[18]

In doing so, we begin to generate change and alternative knowledges or stories about ourselves, our lives and God. These unique knowledges in turn challenge the power and control of our dominant story. The new stories can be performed in words through

---

15 Ibid., p. 31.
16 Ibid., p. 63.
17 Ibid., p. 55.
18 Ibid., p. 56.

writing letters or stories, or speaking them out loud to another person, or by praying to God. They can incorporate the use of analogy to shift our thinking, and they can also be informed by our reading of God's word.

This narrative process is what Tris, from the Divergent series, underwent. She began to re-story and re-author the events in her life when she realised that her divergence was not a thing to conceal and hide, a negative point of difference, but was rather a gift she could use to transform her society for the better. She began to see that many of the events in her life were actually out of her control and were not her fault. Her ability to see this and change inspired other people around her to not give into their pain or run from it, but instead find another purpose to live for. At the end of the last book in the series, Tris' close friend Tobias speaks about the suffering and pain he feels at losing her and the challenge of moving forward despite it.

> *There are so many ways to be brave in this world. Sometimes bravery involves laying down your life for something bigger than yourself, or for someone else. Sometimes it involves giving up everything you have ever known, or everyone you have ever loved, for the sake of something greater.*
>
> *But sometimes it doesn't.*
>
> *Sometimes it is nothing more than gritting your teeth through pain, and the work of every day, the slow walk toward a better life.*
>
> *That is the sort of bravery I must have now.*[19]

The stories below show how the narrative process has the potential to take a story of suffering and redeem it by opening up an entirely new view of life. For the people I interviewed, this process

---

19 Roth, *Allegiant*, p. 509.

was often informed by their faith and the work of God in their life. You might find some of their experiences encouraging.

In the following chapters, we will consider the impact of Jesus' death and resurrection on our stories. As examples, we explore the narratives of the theologian Jurgen Moltmann and the apostle Paul, and how the good news of Jesus Christ re-authored their story and led to radical transformation. We will also look at how allegory as well as linear models of faith development[20] can provide us with additional scaffolding to creatively wrestle with our narratives of suffering.

JAMES: HAVING A CHILD WITH A SEVERE DISABILITY

I thought disaster had struck again, and I counted up all the bad things that had already happened – the bullying at school, Dad dying when I was 10 years old, my insecurities and disappointments. I ruminated about the past. When I felt no hope, I found a way to keep openly acknowledging that although I had no faith, God could give faith to me. I would go on walks and pray raw, angry prayers, but these would end with a short confession of God's goodness like the psalms. The story changed a little bit over time. I got treatment for my underlying anxiety and depression and became more emotionally resilient.

---

20   For a definition and explanation of linear models of faith development, see Chapter 9.

KIM: HAVING A SAME SEX-ATTRACTED CHILD

I had a clear picture of myself and my husband standing at a lookout with parts of the landscape hidden. God picked us up and placed us in another place with a new experience. He did this to teach us something. It was not our own choice. Since then, I have been reading a lot so that I can see things from a different perspective as a different landscape. God took me down a road I hadn't thought about. It was a relief to be freed from the narrative that there's only one correct way of looking at things. I now see that there are a lot more people struggling with the same situation and who can't openly talk about it. This is why the dominant narrative is louder. I am aware of how language can be hurtful and exclude people.

MICHAEL: MINISTRY BURNOUT

I thought, 'I'm wrong, it's my fault, I'm a bad leader, I'm responsible.' I questioned my identity as a follower of Christ and didn't know if my faith would survive. I am more generous to myself now and see the cause and effect of my experience. I have worked through the process of forgiveness. I have rewritten what happened as a learning experience. It was not all about me.

PHOEBE: PARENTING A CHILD WITH A SERIOUS MENTAL ILLNESS

I am such a bad mother. What have I done? If it wasn't for my husband I'd be in a loony bin. I felt guilt about what genetics I had passed on. What about me? I compared myself to other families. I couldn't go to the shops like other people and had to go by myself. I withdrew from people who had normal children and normal lives. I couldn't be bothered explaining. I screamed at my friend, 'You don't understand!' The story got rewritten slowly over time. I learned to stop and be and go deeper into God, learning by teaching other skills and learning them myself. I got my own support and counselling. My husband reframed the situation and focused on the positives. In the last couple of years, I could breathe. She's grown up, moved out of home, and I have more balance and time for myself.

RICHARD: DEATH OF A GRANDCHILD

I reflected on her having a moment in worship at church on stage and she just froze. She said, 'I saw angels.' The month before she died, she came into her parents' bedroom and said, 'There's an angel in my bedroom.' One week before her death, she said to my wife how much she loved her, and it seemed like a deliberate conversation. After her death, I reflected on these things and wondered how this worked, and how angels were preparing her and us. When she died the family gathered in the room, and her mother's immediate reaction was thankfulness, and that God is in control. Even though I don't understand and it didn't take away my pain, it did silence my questions.

ENGAGING IN THE DISCIPLINE OF SUFFERING: EXPRESS YOUR PAIN

Exercise 1: Your dominant story

Try to describe your dominant story about your suffering. How would you describe the problem that has caused your pain? Do this either by writing it down, sitting to quietly reflect on it, or talking it through with someone you trust. You might also find some of these other ideas helpful:

- Write a letter to your younger self.
- Write a letter about how you feel.
- List your disappointments and the ways your problem has impacted you.
- Write a letter/prayer to God about how you feel.

Think about what you might call your problem. Like my friend, you might want to refer to your depression by using a name, such as Susan. Then you can tell your family that Susan is giving you a hard time, so they understand you are having a bad day. This helps clearly communicate you are struggling without attributing it to a personal deficiency. It is equally helpful sometimes just to name the problem as being *the depression*. What might be a good option for a name that might assist you to externalise your problem?

Exercise 2. Embarking on the re-storying

Reflect on times in your life when your problem did not dominate who you were or how you lived. Start to look for exceptions by answering these questions:

- What was different?
- What kind of person were you?
- What did you hold as important?

- What gave you purpose and hope?
- Who supported you and loved you?
- What inspired you?
- Where was God in your experience?

Take the personal strengths, hopes and dreams, and other things you discovered a step further. Write a letter to yourself that lists all the strengths, skills and abilities you used in the alternate story that you have discovered. The letter could be:

- written with compassion to your younger self, based on what you know now
- a list of all the things you are that are exceptions to your dominant story
- all about the way God sees you.

Put it somewhere you can read each day.

To help you with this task, I have provided an example below:

Today might feel horrible, but it won't be like this forever.

Everyone has bad moments.

I can adapt and keep loving forward.

I can recover.

I am strong.

I can get my life together.

I know what I want and what I don't want.

I can accept it when other people don't understand.

And let it go ...

7
The Narrative of the Suffering Christ

When I was 14 years old and in constant physical pain, my faith in God became real and I began to depend on God for everything. I believe that this was because I knew Christ was my brother in suffering, and he understood my struggle. My faith and my pain became intertwined in my life narrative.

I am not alone in my experience of finding comfort in a God who cares about me and understands my pain. Throughout history, people have reassessed their faith and their understanding of God when confronted by overwhelming suffering – think of the Holocaust and racial genocides in Cambodia, Rwanda and Bosnia in the twentieth century; and the senseless acts of terrorism, war and environmental degradation of the twenty-first century. Whatever the context, intense and unprecedented suffering often prompts us to rethink life and its meaning.

Theologians have reconsidered how the death and resurrection of Christ and his suffering help us find meaning in our experiences of both personal and collective pain. In doing so, they have found new ways of making sense of how a trinitarian God could willingly choose to act through the death and resurrection of the Son of God, and how a God of love is impacted by our suffering.

This shift in thinking is important. Our theological emphasis can often be on a God who is all powerful, divine, sovereign and unchanging (i.e. immutable). This is comforting when we feel like we are in the middle of a storm because there is something that is stable when everything else is in a state of flux. It reassures us that God is dependable, no matter what our circumstances. But this thinking offers less consolation if we take it a step further and view God as distant and unable to share in our suffering (i.e. impassible). Such a view portrays God as a cold, immovable rock, illustrating the danger of using just one metaphor to capture the entirety of who God is.

God's unchanging dependability only holds reassurance to us in our pain when it is paired with our knowledge that God also loves, and this was why Christ died on the cross for us (John 3:16). In the cross, we find the ultimate expression of God's love. The mystery of the cross is that God took on our collective suffering, participated in it, and experienced it through the death of his son. But there was no rush from Good Friday to Sunday. There was an in-between of pain and loss that far exceeds anything we might experience in our lives. God did not bypass the suffering or remain untouched by it. Unbelievably, he chose to participate in it in order to get to Sunday, and the redemption, new life and hope of the resurrection.

God is a god of relationship and love. It is not possible for God to love and not be untouched by the object of his love. Love is both part of God's divine character and something God actively does. This makes God vulnerable to experiencing pain in a similar way to us – for example, when we choose to love another person but the relationship breaks down. This is because pain is an inevitable part of what it means to be in relationship. Although we can experience joy, friendship, acceptance and belonging, we can also get hurt and feel loss, betrayal, heartache and disappointment. We remain ourselves, but the experience of suffering impacts us and demands a response from us. If the relationship breaks down, we need to enter a process of forgiveness so that it is restored again.

The good news is that we are not alone when we are faced with senseless suffering in relationships, or when it is caused by poverty, despair, violence and the destruction of creation. God sees and feels what we do. In the midst of this suffering, God provides hope that one day, all of these situations will be redeemed (Rom 8).

This chapter explores how innovations in theological thinking can inform our understanding of suffering in a way that is not dissimilar to the process of restorying in narrative therapy.

The overwhelming suffering experienced by both humanity and creation has resulted in a problem-saturated view of our existence – one that when paired with postmodern nihilism, is devoid of hope. In this context, a narrow emphasis on the unchanging nature of God is inadequate to address the problem. We need to be free to find new meaning by exploring fresh narratives about God and the world – ones that emphasise God's love for the world and his capacity to understand our suffering.

As an example of this process, we are going to explore the life and work of the theologian Jurgen Moltmann, who challenged the church's narrative about the suffering of Christ. Moltmann's innovation in thinking was a direct result of the suffering and pain he was exposed to in World War II. His conversion to Christianity shows how a person can move from a problem-saturated life to one with new meaning and purpose – a change made possible when he realised that Christ is our brother in suffering. The restorying did not stop there, though. Moltmann's theology of the cross brings the death and resurrection of Christ to the centre of faith. It understands God as standing in solidarity with all people, and all of creation, in the midst of suffering.

THE STORY OF SUFFERING IN THE LIFE OF MOLTMANN

Moltmann came to faith in Christ when he was a German prisoner of war living in a Scottish labour camp between 1945 and 1948. In his book *The Source of Life*,[1] Moltmann describes the cold despair and tormenting thoughts he was experiencing at the time, brought on by the fact that he had survived the war while many others had lost their lives. There was no reason why he had escaped while others had not. His pre-war dream of studying maths and physics was in pieces, and it had been replaced with haunting, traumatic memories of war, death and fighting.

Not long after he arrived at the camp in 1945, he was also confronted with the images of pictures from the German concentration camps. He became disillusioned about the reason for which he had fought. His love for his country collapsed, and he felt profound shame and a shared disgrace with his fellow Germans that they were part of what had happened. For the first time in his life, he cried out to God and went on a search for meaning.

---

1 Moltmann, *The Source of Life*, pp. 1–9.

Moltmann was able to re-story his life from humiliation to hope after being given a Bible by an army chaplain. He found in the book of Psalms a voice for his despair. Moltmann identified with Jesus' cry, 'My God, why have you forsaken me?', and through it began to understand Christ and know that Christ understood him. Christ was 'the divine brother in distress, who takes the prisoners with him on the way to resurrection.'[2] This gave him hope, peace and courage to live. He says:

> *This early fellowship with Jesus, the brother in suffering and the redeemer from guilt, has never left me since. I never 'decided for Christ' as is often demanded of us, but I am sure that then and there, in the dark pit of my soul, he found me. Christ's God-forsakenness showed me where God is, where he had been with me in my life, and where he would be in the future.*[3]

Moltmann experienced kindness, grace and forgiveness, and also reconciliation from the Scottish people he lived among and through a group of Dutch Christians who took the initiative to share their wartime experiences. This was liberating. Living in the camp became like a monastic experience, where he had the opportunity to look inward and time to read, learn and question. He immersed himself in books and classes on theology, biblical studies and language, and for the first time attended chapel and listened to sermons. Through this experience, 'what looked like a grim fate when it began turned into an undeserved, rich blessing.'[4] In the words of Psalm 30:11, 'You turned my wailing into dancing.'

Moltmann's theology of the cross centres around the paradox of God being present with the godless. In our despair and pain, we

---

2   Ibid., p. 5.
3   Ibid., p. 5.
4   Ibid., p. 8.

feel abandoned; it feels like God is distant and does not care. But the theology of the cross declares that it is precisely in this darkest time that God is present and feels our hopelessness and loneliness with us. God is present in our desolation. As Psalm 139:12 reminds us: 'even the darkness will not be dark to you; the night will shine like the day, for darkness is as light to you.'

This is the restorying. Even though we might feel alone, God has not left us. He is right in the middle of our desolation. *Knowing* this – in our mind and spirit – has the power to transform our experience of our situation, so it brings us closer to God, not further away.

Moltmann's lived experience and transformed understanding of God brought about one of the most radical and influential theological shifts in how we, as a church, see Christ. In fact, Moltmann's work continues to influence us even now. It replaced the long-held idea that God does not change with an understanding that while the essential aspects of God's character and nature remain the same, God through his love feels our pain and is impacted by it.[5] At the core, God is trinitarian and relational, not cold and distant and benevolent. God cares when his creation suffers, and he understands injustice and pain. This new knowledge re-storied not just Moltmann's life, but our collective understanding of God. We are now going to explore his thinking further.

THE SYMBOL OF THE CROSS

Have you ever considered how extraordinary it is that the Christian faith focuses on the death of a man on a cross? The cross is used as

---

5   It is outside the scope of this book to thoroughly cover theological debate about the suffering of God. The reader is referred to Fiddes, P.S. *The Creative Suffering of God*, Clarendon Paperbacks, Oxford, 2002.

the symbol of our faith, yet it is a strange choice considering that in the time of Jesus, the Roman Empire used crucifixion as a punishment for slaves and people who rebelled against their rule. It was a degrading punishment. From a Roman perspective, therefore, any religious movement that used the cross as its symbol was somehow perverse.[6] And, from the Jewish perspective, this same cross implied that the person was excluded from the covenant of life, condemned by the law, and excluded from the fellowship of God.[7]

The disciples must have felt that Jesus' death was the end of his claim to be the Messiah. They would have had no concept of a Messiah, a bringer of salvation, condemned to death (Luke 23:2). What happened to their Teacher was shameful beyond belief,[8] and this is why they fled the scene of the crucifixion. They had no reason to keep their faith because everything they had believed in had come to nothing.

It is not until after the resurrection that the disciples were able to reconstruct, or re-story, who they thought Jesus was. Jesus had actually asked them who they thought he was before his death. Peter had answered, 'You are the Messiah [the Christ], the Son of the living God' (Matt 16:16). On the Friday, the day of his crucifixion, all hope of this had left them – until they met the resurrected Jesus on the Sunday.

So, for early Christians, the cross was a truly strange symbol around which to build their faith, especially because at the time the people around them thought their worship of a crucified God was inappropriate and even blasphemous.

---

6 Moltmann, *The Source of Life*, p. 40.
7 Ibid., p. 39.
8 Ibid., pp. 190–191.

And the conundrum of the cross persists today. From a humanistic point of view, it remains peculiar unless we follow Moltmann's rationale that Jesus' death on the cross makes sense if we understand him to be Jesus Christ both crucified and risen.[9]

Yet in the church we have grown somewhat oblivious to this controversy. We have become used to the cross and are dulled to its significance. Moltmann argues against this mindset, because 'the cross is the centre of all Christian theology.'[10] He goes further to say that the symbol of the cross is an invitation to understand the Christ as the 'outstretched God of the Trinity.'[11] All of our understanding of God is to be found in the events of Christ's death and resurrection.[12]

Moltmann argues that this symbol invites a change of mind, heart, ethics and lifestyle. It pushes us out to fellowship with and meet the pain of the marginalised, oppressed and abandoned. It invites those same oppressed people into fellowship with a crucified God.[13] These two things are held in tension. When we forget them, the image of the cross ceases to be a symbol and becomes instead a meaningless idol.

THE SUFFERING OF GOD

It is Moltmann's view that God suffers in the suffering of Christ. He rejects the old idea of an uninvolved, insensitive being who cannot be moved by anything, and he replaces it with a God who is impacted by injustice and suffering, and who loves.[14] This suffering

---

9   Ibid., p. 226.
10   Ibid., p. 293.
11   Ibid., p. 299.
12   Ibid., p. 295.
13   Ibid., p. 51.
14   Ibid., p. 324.

God is found in the suffering Christ on the cross, who cries out 'My God, why have you forsaken me?' Just as God loves, he also suffers, and these concepts are interrelated.[15] To love someone means to actively open yourself up to the possibility of pain.[16] God chooses this way because he is a God of love.

When placed in the context of the Trinity, Moltmann's understanding of the cross pushes us to hold these two opposite ideas in tension – in the same way we hold other truths about God. For example, God is both divine and human, simultaneously.

Importantly for Moltmann, the death of the Son does not equate to the death of God. Instead, the death of the Son (and the grief of the Father) is the God event in which the life-giving Spirit of love emerges.[17] In this way, the cross – the death and resurrection of Christ – is the event at the very centre of our understanding of who God is. It makes sense of all events that occurred before and after it. And it places the Trinity in context.

So, when we suffer and cry out to God in our distress and forsakenness, we are echoing the death cry of the dying Christ, the Son of God. The Christ we pray to is a human God who understands our pain and intercedes for us. The reality of our humanity is that the more we love, the more we open ourselves to both happiness and pain. To love means to live, and to suffer. 'In this way we experience life and death in love.'[18]

When Christ went to the cross, he suffered abandonment and rejection by God, his Father. He took on the eternal death of the

---

15 Ibid., p. 332.
16 Ibid., p. 337.
17 Ibid., p. 373.
18 Ibid., p. 374.

forsaken and Godless so that they could commune with God. This means that there is no loneliness or rejection that he did not take upon himself on the cross.[19] Our God understands our experience and has held our pain.

The suffering of the crucified Christ speaks to people in pain. 'Through his own abandonment by God, the crucified Christ brings God to those abandoned by God. Through his suffering he brings salvation to those who suffer. Through his death he brings eternal life to those who are dying.'[20]

Somehow, we identify in the crucified Christ our own pain and know that he understands. To follow this crucified Christ means to be a brother or sister with him in this suffering. To take up our cross and follow means that we will be imitators of his suffering[21] and enter the rejection and scandal of the cross in our own life.

The reason this is relevant to us here and now in our own pain, and the pain of our world, is that our suffering is transformed by the resurrection. The resurrected Jesus Christ brings us new life and creates change. It is the spark of a new era that we are invited to participate in. We have new life; God transforms us, and we become agents of transformation within the world. The resurrection of the suffering Christ is the restorying of the suffering world – redemption.

The hope, then, that the cross provides is that the crucified God has embraced and overcome the world, and that love is more powerful than death.[22]

---

19   Ibid., p. 414.
20   Ibid., pp. 61–62.
21   Ibid., p. 69.
22   Ibid., p. 417.

Brotherhood with Christ means the suffering and active participation in the history of this God. Its criterion is the history of the crucified and risen Christ. Its power is the sighing and liberating spirit of God. Its consummation lies in the kingdom of the triune God which sets all things free and fills them with meaning.[23]

For me, Moltmann provides hope in our dark places, because he writes of a God who knows and feels our pain in the cross but does not abandon us there. God promises new life and a future in the resurrection, to redeem our suffering so that it is not pointless. That is why Paul's statement that 'in all things God works for the good of those who love him, who have been called according to his purpose' is true (Rom 8:28). The resurrection redeems our brokenness and pain. Moltmann has provided us with a new way of understanding the good news of Christ: Jesus Christ is our brother in suffering and the redeemer of our pain and that of the world.

My pathway to faith was not through seeing myself as a sinner who needed forgiveness. Rather, it was by finding in God love and understanding in my suffering, and through trust in him, transformation of my life. This did not mean the healing of my physical pain. I still live with this each day. God's grace gives me courage to live despite it. But I have been transformed, and I hold onto the hope that one day I will be free of pain when I am with God in eternity.

Likewise, many of the people I interviewed for this book related similar experiences. They said that the death and resurrection of Christ informed their suffering and anchored their faith. It helped them feel less alone. It gave them hope.

---

23   Ibid., p. 494.

BROOKE: ABANDONMENT IN MARRIAGE

God knows all my feelings. We will never understand the depth of suffering, the depth of our sin or the depth of his love. My suffering is small in comparison to what Christ went through.

JAMES: HAVING A CHILD WITH A SEVERE DISABILITY

There is a future and hope for my son as a child of God, redeemed by God. He will get a new body. There is hope for him. Meanwhile, the resurrection power gives me strength to keep going.

JOSHUA: YOUTH STRUGGLING WITH FAITH

The cross gave me an important perspective of Christ's suffering at the hands of others. I recognised why it was important for the suffering of myself and other people. I experienced the dying of my naive dreams, and since then the resurrection has brought depth to my ministry and the way I spend time with people.

KARLY: MINISTRY LOSS

It was a slow, disappointing death of my dream role in a dream team. The people in my new job were affirming and asked my opinion about things. This was healing, and like a process of coming back to life. I now have a calmer passion for ministry.

KIM: HAVING A SAME SEX-ATTRACTED CHILD

No matter how grey faith gets, the death and resurrection of Christ is an anchor and central to faith, a focal point.

MICHAEL: MINISTRY BURNOUT

The cross is important to provide perspective – Christ suffering at the hands of others. Recognising why the cross is important, suffering for me and others. Jesus saying 'God, why have you forsaken me?' was my fault too. At the time, my focus was on the past and the dying of my naive dreams rather than the resurrection. Now my emphasis is on the resurrection, and this has brought depth to my ministry and how I spend time with people.

RICHARD: DEATH OF A GRANDCHILD

I have certainty that there is life after death because I believe Jesus is the resurrection and the life. I have moments of pain, but wind blows through unexpectedly and leaves only the pain of missing her.

ENGAGING IN THE DISCIPLINE OF SUFFERING: CHRIST, BROTHER IN SUFFERING

Exercise 1. The symbol of the cross

Sometimes on Palm Sunday people make a small cross out of a simple reed, folded carefully to symbolise the death and resurrection of Christ. One of my counselling clients gave me a cross like this during Lent, and I put it on my desk to keep my life and work centred on Christ. When I reflect on this special gift, it is both fitting and significant because my office is a place where I am privileged to sit with people who are wrestling with life's deep issues.

Make a simple cross from a reed or a piece of paper. There are a number of websites that provide instructions for how to do this.[24]

Do this silently and meditatively. When it is complete, sit and focus on your cross and contemplate the significance of the death and resurrection of Christ, and what this means for your pain and suffering. What comfort or hope does it provide and why?

Exercise 2. Meditate on the Easter story

Read Matthew chapters 27 and 28, and enter into the story. Pretend you are an observer of the events as they happened. Imagine in your mind what the scene must have been like, the sounds and sights and smells. Really engage with the story and what it would have been like to witness the crucifixion and resurrection of Christ. Imagine what it would have been like for Jesus to suffer as he did. Then reflect on the significance of the cross and what this means in your life and for your suffering.

---

24 See, for example, UCatholic, 'How to Make a Palm Cross', 14 April 2019, https://ucatholic.com/blog/palm-cross-instructions/

8
The Narrative of the Apostle Paul

The life of the apostle Paul provides another insight into the strength of narrative in rewriting our story of ourselves and God in light of the death and resurrection of Christ.

Meeting Christ on the road to Damascus was an event that changed Paul's world and how he saw himself. It brought about an internal and external transformation – one so marked that it was signified by a change in name, from Saul to Paul.

For Paul, life as a follower of Jesus is a journey towards being Christlike. And the problems and pain we encounter along the way are an opportunity for God to work in our lives in amazing and powerful ways. Following Jesus means identifying with the suffering of the cross and the power of the resurrection – we die to ourselves and live in God's redemptive power as a new creation. In Paul's theology we discover the great mystery that God's power is made perfect in our weakness (2 Cor 12:9), and that we do not have to rely on our own strength to be a messenger of transformation, a carrier of the light of Christ.

Paul's story is somewhat unique, because in the New Testament we have the opportunity to see it both through the eyes of Luke and also Paul's personal account of what he experienced during his conversion, journey of faith and ministry to the early church.

THE NARRATIVE OF PAUL FROM THE PERSPECTIVE OF LUKE

Paul first appears in the book of Acts as the young man named Saul who watched and approved of the stoning of Stephen, outside Jerusalem (Acts 7:54–60). Saul, along with other religious groups that included the members of the Sanhedrin (religious council) and factions of the Jewish faith, had been angered because Stephen made a theological case for his faith that they believed was blasphemous against Moses and God (Acts 6:11) and a threat to their customs and teachings (Acts 6:14). Stephen had also made accusations against them directly –'You are just like your ancestors: you always resist the Holy Spirit!' – and claimed that they had betrayed and murdered the Messiah (Acts 7:51–53).

Stephen's stoning was the event that marked the start of a severe persecution against the early church, which scattered the apostles throughout Judea and Samaria. 'Saul began to destroy the church. Going from house to house, he dragged off both men and women and put them in prison' (Acts 8:3). Then, 'breathing out murderous threats against the Lord's disciples' (Acts 9:1), Saul went to Caiaphas the high priest to ask for letters of introduction to the synagogue in Damascus, which was 225 kms to the northeast of Jerusalem, to ask for support in arresting any followers of the Way that had escaped the initial persecution. His intention was to bring them back to the capital to face the same kind of trial as Stephen.

It was while Saul was approaching Damascus that a 'light from heaven flashed around him' and he fell to the ground. He heard a voice say to him,

'Saul, Saul, why do you persecute me?'

'Who are you, Lord?' Saul asked.

'I am Jesus, whom you are persecuting,' he replied. 'Now get up and go into the city, and you will be told what you must do' (Acts 9:3–6).

The men travelling with him were speechless because they heard the voice but could not see anyone. When Saul got up from the ground he was blind, and the men had to lead him by the hand to Damascus. For three days he was unable to see, and he neither ate nor drank.

God had turned Saul's life upside down in an instant. He had thought he was being zealously faithful to God in his persecution of the followers of the Way, but he discovered that he was mistaken. He was, in fact, persecuting Christ and working against God. In Acts 5:39, Gamaliel, a teacher of the law, had argued that if the Way was not from God, then it would peter out in its own time. But if it was from God, then they would not be able to oppose it and to do so would be the same as fighting against God.

After Saul's arrival in Damascus, God spoke to a disciple called Ananias in a vision and said, 'Go to the house of Judas on Straight Street and ask for a man from Tarsus named Saul, for he is praying. In a vision he has seen a man named Ananias come and place his hands on him to restore his sight' (Acts 9:11–12).

Ananias's response is not that surprising: 'Lord ... I have heard many reports about this man and all the harm he has done to your holy people in Jerusalem. And he has come here with authority from the chief priests to arrest all who call on your name' (Acts 9:13–14).

God encouraged Ananias to go regardless, for 'this man is my chosen instrument to proclaim my name to the Gentiles and their kings and to the people of Israel. I will show him how much he must suffer for my name' (Acts 9:15–16).

So, despite his well-placed fear, Ananias did what he was asked. He laid his hands on Saul and prayed for him so that his sight would be restored and he would be filled with the Holy Spirit.

This miraculous conversion marked the start of Saul's ministry. He now went to the synagogues to tell people Jesus was the Son of God, to the shock of all who heard him. They said, 'Isn't the man who caused havoc in Jerusalem among those who call on this name? And hasn't he come here to take them as prisoners to the chief priests?' (Acts 9:21). Many in Damascus were somewhat confused by this about-turn, and it was not long before some of them plotted to kill Saul and he had to escape the city at night by being lowered in a basket through an opening in the city wall. He was now being treated the same way he had once treated the disciples.

The key change in Saul's thinking was his realisation that Jesus was the Messiah and the scriptures had been fulfilled. He did not convert to a new religion, but remained loyal to the God of Israel whom he had always served. Grasping that God's coming in the form of Jesus the Messiah was a world-changing reality for him.[1]

When Saul tried to join with the disciples, they were deeply afraid of him because they found it hard to believe that he had had a genuine change of heart. It took the hard work of Barnabas to convince the apostles to listen to Saul and hear his amazing conversion story.

It was not long before Saul found himself arguing with the same group of Jews who had killed Stephen. After hearing that these Jews planned to kill Saul, the other believers sent Saul to Tarsus, the town where he was from.

---

1 Wright, *Paul: A Biography*, p. 54.

According to N.T. Wright, for the next 10 years Saul went silent. Luke does not include any detail about what happened to him,[2] but it is likely that he worked in the family business as a tentmaker. Wright argues that this time would have been spiritually formative for Saul as he reflected on his understanding of Jesus the Messiah and how this fitted into his understanding of God.[3]

We can infer quite a bit about his pondering. From everything we know of Saul of Tarsus, on the one hand, and Paul the Apostle, on the other, we cannot imagine that in this early period he ever stopped thinking things through, soaking that reflection in Jewish-style prayer, focusing it on Israel's scriptures, and, like many other devout diaspora Jews, engaging with the culture all around him. He searched the ancient scriptures for all he was worth and argued about them in the synagogue and at the workbench with his friends and family. He thought his way backward from the 'new fact', as he saw it, of a crucified and risen Messiah, back into the world of Israel's scriptures and traditions, back into the long, dark, and often twisted narrative of Israel that had been groping its way forward to that point without glimpsing its true goal ... With hindsight ... he saw Jesus all over the place – not arbitrarily ... but as the infinite point where the parallel lines of Israel's long narrative would eventually meet.[4]

This period of reflection would have allowed time for Saul's thinking to mature and form a coherent Christian theology. It is interesting that it was after his time in Tarsus that Saul became known and recognised as a prophet and teacher who was set apart to proclaim the word of God. And it was at this point that he became known as the apostle Paul.

---

2   Ibid., p. 68.
3   Ibid., p. 69.
4   Ibid., pp. 70–71.

What I find interesting about this is that Paul's period of silence was a fundamental part of God's redemption in his story. My observation is this often happens to us after a great loss or time of intense suffering. We go inward, and we wrestle with our problem. We need time and space for God to work in our pain and transform and teach us before we are ready to go back out into the world again and show the redeeming work of God in our lives.

THE REWRITING OF PAUL'S NARRATIVE ACCORDING TO LUKE

The Gospel of Luke presents us with two different perspectives on Saul. The first, through the eyes of the disciples and believers of the Way, saw Saul as a persecutor of the church, a person to be feared, a doer of evil who breathed threats of murder against them. The second, through God's eyes, saw him as someone who would take the good news of Jesus far and wide – and that he would suffer for this.

Just imagine if Paul had got stuck in the first narrative that he was evil and to be feared. The reactions of the other disciples could have fed into his understanding of himself, and he could have fixated on being rejected by the church and given up on ministry. However, several things came together to spur him on. He had met Christ on the road to Damascus, Ananias gave him a chance, Barnabas could see the possibility of a new Saul, and he spent an extended time in reflection consolidating his theology. He was indeed a new creation (2 Cor 5:17). His life had been re-storied, and he could build a new future and purpose on this knowledge of himself. He literally had a new name and identity: Paul the apostle.

I find it curious that God specifically said that Paul's new purpose was to preach the good news but also to suffer (Acts 9:15–16). This is possibly not the most heartening mission to be given. Yet we see that Paul embraces this suffering as going hand in hand with his faith.

PAUL'S NARRATIVE AND UNDERSTANDING OF SUFFERING

Philippians 3:4b–11 gives us some insight into how Paul viewed his conversion and the redirection of his life. Although he used to identify as a Jewish Pharisee and a persecutor of the church, his efforts to live that life to perfection were now of no worth to him. His social status, academic accomplishments and personal ambition were no longer important. Instead, he valued his relationship with Christ, which was based on faith rather than his achievements. Paul made a clear choice to turn away from the person he used to be and start on a new course. His values had changed and become those of the kingdom of God, consistent with the teachings of Jesus of Nazareth, the Christ.

There exists a great mystery and power in a life totally surrendered to God – one where a person's will is completely aligned with God's. It is the path that our faith leads us down, and it is the path that suffering takes us on. Without the hardship, we would not learn the important and hard-to-grasp lesson that the experience of suffering is part of becoming like Christ, identifying with a death to self so that we can have life and a relationship with God. Rather than adversity breaking us under the strain, we find freedom to live in the power of the resurrection, with new life, as a new creation.

In 2 Corinthians Paul expands on how a life of faith is intertwined with suffering, encouraging us that 'since through God's mercy we have this ministry, we do not lose heart' (2 Cor 4:1). He says that he does not proclaim himself, but Jesus Christ as Lord. It is God who shines his light within our hearts so other people can know God through Christ. This emphasises God acting through us, rather than anything we do ourselves. We hold the treasure of the light of Christ, the message of the good news, in ordinary clay jars – containers that are not beautiful and do not attract attention. And so, people don't notice us, but they are attracted to the power of God within us. None of this is due to our own effort, skill or gifting. We are just the vessel.

Paul goes on to say that in carrying this light and message, he has been afflicted, perplexed, persecuted and struck down, but he has never given up (2 Cor 4:7). The suffering is a way of identifying with the death of Jesus, and death of self, so that the life of Jesus is visible within him. The resurrection power is the light of Christ. Once again he says, 'so we do not lose heart' (2 Cor 4:16).

From Paul's account, his life was anything but easy. He names his sufferings:

> *Five times I received from the Jews the forty lashes minus one. Three times I was beaten with rods, once I was pelted with stones, three times I was shipwrecked, I spent a night and a day in the open sea, I have been constantly on the move. I have been in danger from rivers, in danger from bandits, in danger from my fellow Jews, in danger from Gentiles; in danger in the city, in danger in the country, in danger at sea; and in danger from false believers. I have laboured and toiled and have often gone without sleep; I have known hunger and thirst and have often gone without food; I have been cold and naked. Besides everything else, I face daily the pressure of my concern for all the churches (2 Cor 11:24–28).*

He also mentions his own personal struggle with a 'thorn in my flesh' (2 Cor 12:7), the details of which we can only speculate about. Paul asked God three times to take this problem from him, and his prayer was not answered. God's response was, 'My grace is sufficient for you, for my power is made perfect in weakness' (2 Cor 12:9). This reveals that Paul genuinely struggled. His life was not easy. Yet he kept going, finding that it was his very weakness that God graciously used to be his greatest asset.

PAUL'S THEOLOGY OF SUFFERING

Paul, in his deep reflection on his own life and suffering, offers us a new way of seeing ourselves in dark times. His personal narrative gives us some key insights that can be an encouragement to us. Like Paul,

* following Christ means we have died to ourselves
* our old life has gone and our new life has come
* our narrative needs to change
* we are new creations in Christ
* we live in a new world of possibility empowered by the Holy Spirit.

Paul argues that it is God who is working within us, and radically, 'though outwardly we are wasting away, yet inwardly we are being renewed day by day' (2 Cor 4:16). There is a deep transformation taking place within us when we suffer – one that involves our physical life, 'what is mortal', being 'swallowed up by life' (2 Cor 5:4). This is the plan God had for us all along, and the Holy Spirit lives and acts within us to this purpose (2 Cor 5:5). This is why God does not take all our problems away. Having a burden to carry through life, like a thorn in the flesh, can help orientate us to God so that our weaknesses become strengths and we do not rely on our own innate ability to do things.

Our suffering is a pathway to identification with the death and resurrection of Christ, and our struggles need to be seen in the light of eternity. In this context, it is not surprising that Paul describes our troubles as 'light and momentary' – experiences that prepare us for eternal life with God, as what we live and see and experience now is only temporary, but what we cannot yet see is eternal (2 Cor 4:17–18). From this perspective, it is not much of a leap in thinking to decide that we would rather be with God than here in our body (2 Cor 5:9), which is what Paul writes in Philippians 1:21: 'For to me, to live is Christ and to die is gain.' He is actually seeing his life from a whole new perspective – that of eternity. The new life in Christ that has started already and will continue forever. We no longer live for ourselves, but for Christ who died and was raised again (2 Cor 5:15).

APPLICATION OF PAUL'S NARRATIVE TO OUR LIVES

I wonder if we become numb to the experience of Paul's life and ministry because we have heard these stories so many times. It no longer challenges our thinking. This is disappointing, because Paul shares with us a message of redemption and hope that can carry us through our pain. He says:

> *Therefore, since we have been justified through faith, we have peace with God through our Lord Jesus Christ, through whom we have gained access by faith into this grace in which we now stand. And we boast in the hope of the glory of God. Not only so, but we also glory in our sufferings, because we know that suffering produces perseverance; perseverance, character; and character, hope. And hope does not put us to shame, because God's love has been poured out into our hearts through the Holy Spirit, who has been given to us (Rom 5:1–5).*

Paul's life is like a prototype of what is possible for us. His belief and surrender to Christ gave him a new name and a new identity, and it made it possible to re-story his life. Suffering was a key part of this process. It gave him purpose, and it transformed him and forced him to rely on God to sustain him in everything he did. His message became one of hope and redemption.

This has certainly been the case in my own life. The problems I have had to face, while painful at the time, have been transformative because my suffering pushes me to rely on God. My selfishness and control are stripped back. Sometimes I have thought that things would never improve. But I have found that God is faithful, and he redeems my life and my circumstances in time. I become more Christlike and develop a more godly character. When I despair, this turns to hope because Christ is with me.

JAMES: PARENT OF A CHILD WITH A SEVERE DISABILITY

The resurrection power gives strength to sustain our family. We are not just dependent on our personal resources. In Romans 8 it talks about the resurrection power flowing out into our physical realm.

JOSHUA: YOUTH STRUGGLING WITH FAITH

Paul says we are saved by grace and grace alone – because whenever I make mistakes and doubt my worth, it gives me greater confidence because it is not about what I do.

God already did everything through the death and resurrection, so it is all about continuing God's work. It's not our works but God's works that give us salvation. God says he desires mercy and not sacrifice. In my cynicism I saw the world as power. This is a reminder to not be so cynical, as it is all about God. Sacrifice can make you see yourself as not worthy.

KIM: HAVING A SAME SEX-ATTRACTED CHILD

Suffering has a sacred role in life. If it didn't have purpose, God would spare us.

PHOEBE: PARENTING A CHILD WITH A SERIOUS MENTAL ILLNESS

We will be part of a new creation, and this gives hope and connection to others horizontally, and to God vertically. The narrative of the world, sin and redemption continues with us in it.

ENGAGING IN THE DISCIPLINE OF SUFFERING: LIVING AS A NEW CREATION IN CHRIST

Exercise 1: Mapping your narrative of faith

What are the significant life-changing moments or events where you learned something about yourself and God changed you? For example, a few years ago I was grappling with the decision to quit my job and step out in faith and follow God into the unknown. I read the words of Matthew 7:6, 'Do not give what is holy to dogs; and do not throw your pearls before swine, or they will trample them under foot and turn and maul you'. Later that week I went out for a coffee and chat with a close friend, and to my surprise she quoted this same passage at me without knowing I had been mulling over its meaning for several days. This, plus a couple of other events at that time, encouraged me to take the plunge and leave my job. Your experience might be different. It might have been something someone said, the consequences of an event, the words of a song, or a dream.

- Make a timeline on a piece of paper and mark the events.
- Try to articulate what it was that you think God was saying to you at that time.
- How have you changed?

Reflect on Romans 5:1–5. How has suffering helped you to endure? What new character has it formed within you? How have these things changed the way you see the future and how you love?

Exercise 2: The thorn in your flesh

Paul grappled with a problem that he repeatedly prayed about to God, begging that he take it away. This did not happen. Instead,

God said to him, 'My grace is sufficient for you, for my power is made perfect in weakness' (2 Cor 12:9).

I wonder if you are facing a similar issue in your life. If you can identify what this is, give it a name. Over the next week, start and end the day by surrendering this problem to God and asking him to provide the grace and power to sustain you.

In the past couple of years, I have done this by reading the Suscipe Prayer of Ignatius of Loyola.[5] I found it orientated my mind to the day so that my attitude and perspective were similar to that of Paul, who of course modelled his life on Christ. I have modernised the words.

Lord take my entire freedom,
My memory,
My understanding,
My whole will.
All that I am and own,
You have given to me:
I surrender it all to you so you can use it for your will.
I only need your love and grace;
With these I will be rich enough and desire nothing else.
Amen.

---

5 Welborn, 'Suscipe, the Radical Prayer'.

9
Narratives that Externalise and Transform Our Faith and Suffering

I t is rare to struggle with just one problem in life. There are times when we wonder if all the pain and heartache will ever end. At these times, when we struggle the most, we are often grateful for the precious people who journey with us. This is because we can take comfort in the solidarity of being able to share our stories of struggle together.

I clearly remember sitting at a café with one of my best friends. Over coffee we were sharing the story of our challenges and problems, and trying to make sense of them. At some point in the conversation, we agreed that saying 'things can't possibly get any worse' was rather stupid because things often did. This was a profound moment of realisation.

Since this conversation, my friend and I sometimes give each other a knowing look and joke about where our lives are at, because we have learned that the avalanche of struggles and pain can keep coming at us and push us to the point where we think we might break. It has been our faith in God, love for each other and shared experiences that have brought us through these tough times.

In his award-winning book *The Narrow Road to the Deep North*, Richard Flanagan writes, 'A happy man has no past, while an unhappy man has nothing else.'[1] This is so true, because each of us in our personal history has some kind of scar from a physical or emotional injury that we have sustained. No matter who we are, we cannot completely escape suffering. We need to grow through it.

Allegory and story, and linear models of faith development, are tools that assist us to move beyond our suffering to find an alternative path or way to understand our situation and where God fits into it. This is so important because without these aids to our journey, we often get lost in our pain and have a tendency to stay there or become deformed by it. I often revisit Hebrews 12:12, because it serves as a warning to me to not go back to those places in my internal narrative that reinforce the pain I have lived through. I need to keep moving forward. 'Therefore, strengthen your feeble arms and weak knees. "Make level paths for your feet", so that the lame may not be disabled, but rather healed' (Heb 12:12–13).

I am also sure that this is why Paul writes, 'forgetting what is behind and straining towards what is ahead, I press on towards the goal to win the prize for which God has called me heavenward in Christ Jesus' (Phil 3:13–14).

In moving forward, we need to be careful that we are not running away from our pain. Both allegory and linear models of faith development challenge us at the points where we are tempted to turn

---

1 Flanagan, *The Narrow Road to the Deep North*, p. 3.

backward, or duck for cover and avoid facing holes in our under-standing of self or God. These approaches are not necessarily meant to be read as biblical truth or be theologically flawless. Rather, they offer us a creative tool that uses metaphors for understanding, and models of faith that can challenge the way we see our situation.

In the next section, we take a look at some writers who use these literary methods and have much to teach us about how to sit with pain, make sense of it, externalise it and then find a way forward on a new path that provides us with hope and a future. If we have the courage to embark on this process of discovery that they are inviting us on, we have the opportunity to grow and develop.

LINEAR MODELS OF THE DEVELOPMENT OF FAITH

We begin with two books that are examples of linear models of how to navigate suffering: *Dark Night of the Soul*[2] and *The Critical Journey*.[3] Here, linear model refers to a theory or way of seeing faith which is sequential – it changes and grows with maturity, self-development and our understanding of God.

Both books describe the desperate struggle we go through when we come up against a time in life that seems bleak and unpassable. The challenge is to persevere and get through this time and come out with a new understanding of God that is deeper and based on God's unshakable love.

These models have been a source of deep consolation to many Christians. They normalise our struggle and provide a framework through which we can explore our own faith narrative. In each

---

2   St John of the Cross, 'Dark Night of the Soul'.
3   Hagberg & Guelich, *The Critical Journey*.

case, they provide a way to externalise the problem and then move through it.

One criticism of these linear models is that they assume that life is neat and can be categorised into stages that we move through over time sequentially. This is often not the case, though, as it is possible and often the case that we revisit these dark times, or experience more than one stage of faith simultaneously. The concepts are, however, helpful, and if they are used flexibly, they can encourage us in the Way.

'The Dark Night of the Soul'

St John of the Cross describes how our faith develops and deepens through a twofold process. It begins with a moderate level of suffering as we learn to surrender our sensual desires, in what he calls the *dark night of the senses*. We learn to give up our desires and begin to value communing with God above all else. Over time, our good deeds spring from a right motivation as we begin to care less for appearance and personal gain and more about who God is. We begin to understand ourselves better, detach ourselves from the things around us and commune with God in a more respectful way.[4]

Out of our growing self-knowledge comes a growing knowledge of God.[5] We lose our spiritual pride, we no longer compare ourselves with others and we begin to love other people. St John invites us to consider the examples of Moses and Job. In the presence of God, Moses took his shoes off and did not dare look at him.[6] And, in the depths of misery after everything material had

---

4 St John of the Cross, 'Dark Night of the Soul', Book 1: The Dark Night of Sense, ch. 12.
5 Ibid.
6 Ibid.

been taken from him, Job came to understand his place before God.[7] In the same way, as we grow in our knowledge of God, we become humble and obedient to him.

We also find a new strength – one that grows out of our own weakness. Out of the darkness we find peace, a continual focus on God and a purity of soul.[8] Our soul is purged of wrath, envy and sloth, and instead it becomes quiet and at rest. A new thing starts, where God feeds and refreshes the soul without us actively doing anything. Our soul is 'no longer disturbed and angry with itself because of its own faults, nor with its neighbour because of his, neither is it displeased with God, nor does it utter unseemly complaints because He does not quickly make it holy.[9]

The second stage of suffering described by St John is the *dark night of the spirit*. Here, the change that comes penetrates deeper as God's light shines into the root of our habits, behaviours and attachments. The two parts of the soul – the spiritual and sensual – are completely purged.[10] We are stripped of our thoughts, memories, feelings and pleasures. It is the great letting go of all we hold onto in life to the point where we die a spiritual death.

This whole process is about letting go of the things we hold onto in life – a process that is painful but allows us to fully die to ourselves. We are transformed so that we can love God deeply from a place where we are rid of unhealthy motives and conditions. Over time, our understanding changes so that it no longer comes from ourselves but from Divine wisdom. Love comes from

---

7 Ibid.
8 Ibid., ch. 13.
9 Ibid.
10 St John of the Cross, 'Dark Night of the Soul', Book 2: The Dark Night of the Spirit, ch. 3.

the strength and purity of the Holy Spirit, the will comes from God, and the energy and affection of our soul comes from Divine temper and delight.[11] Through all these things, God is teaching the soul about love – without it having done anything in and of itself to gain this knowledge.

The suffering and pain we feel during this time is magnified by the Divine light, which shines light on our impurity and unhelpful attachments. The pain is often furthered by the false belief that God is against us, or we have set ourselves against God.[12] We can feel like God has sent us away, and we are all alone. It feels like we are carrying an oppressive weight and that no-one really cares – just like Job, who asked for pity.[13] This is despite the fact that in reality, God is gentle. It is not God who is causing this suffering, but in the midst of it, he is working to change us so that our faith and love go deeper than they ever could have before.

It is like we are emptying ourselves so that we are free to live totally for God. The suffering is drawing us away from what we have known so that we move closer to God. In this new place, we discover the inner peace that passes all understanding.[14] We gain Divine love and wisdom. Our strength is renewed[15] and God adds to it, described so well in Isaiah 40:31: 'those who hope in the LORD will renew their strength. They will soar on wings like eagles; they will run and not grow weary, they will walk and not be faint.'

We are clothed like new people. We become purer, wiser and more cautious. We keep our eyes fixed on God and through this

---

11 Ibid., ch. 4.
12 Ibid., ch. 5.
13 Ibid.
14 Ibid., ch. 9.
15 Ibid., ch. 13.

develop faith, hope, love and charity. I would add another characteristic to St John's list here, which is grace.

Out of our suffering, God works in us to change our attitude, motivation, character and orientation to life. We go deeper into the love and wisdom of God. It is God who starts this process passively when we feel most in the midst of darkness, and as we journey further into it, we begin to join with God in this process. All of this time, through the pain and despair, we are moving in love towards God.

This idea of St John's of growing through different stages of refinement in our faith, and externalising the suffering as *the dark night of the senses* and *the dark night of the spirit*, is extremely freeing. We see we are not alone in this struggle, and we are not the first to go through it. In many ways, the first stage of giving up our sensual desires is similar to the concept of repentance. We are leaving everything in life in order to love God and begin the inner transformation that comes from a relationship with him. The second stage is the hard one, as it describes a type of suffering that is characterised by despair and loneliness. This type of pain strips our life back on a deeper level so that all that is left is our relationship with God.

In St John's conceptualisation of life as a follower of Christ, it is when we are at our lowest point that God works in us because we become open to this transformation. Our choice is whether or not we accept the invitation to join in with the work of this transformation of our inner self. I think this is why we often see that people who have been through great suffering and successfully process it are characterised by a deep peace and grace, and a type of love that has no strings attached.

The Critical Journey

The Critical Journey[16] is one of many modern formulations of the stages of faith. I have included it in this section because it is not about achieving growth for its own sake, or to help us become successful super-Christians. Rather, it is more focused on helping us identify where we are and why we might be stuck, and offering a way forward through these difficulties. These stages of faith.

According to this model there are six stages of faith, which are described in Table 2. Briefly, they are

1. the recognition of God
2. the life of discipleship
3. the productive life
4. the journey inward
5. the journey outward
6. the life of love.

Most of us cycle through the stages or revisit a previous stage for a length of time. This is normal.

One of the most informative aspects of this model is the idea of the 'Wall', which is encountered between stages four and five. It is a time of wrestling and transformation that leads to a renewal of faith and healing for people who have the courage to move through it. It is similar to St John's idea of the *dark night of the spirit*. Again, the crisis of suffering is given a name and context, which externalises it and provides a scaffolding within which we can understand it and find some key ways to move forward.

The Wall is a central part of the journey inward, and how we progress through this challenge will determine our level of

---

16   Hagberg & Guelich, *The Critical Journey*.

spiritual healing and transformation, and the extent of renewal of our faith. It is a call to fully surrender our will to God's at the deepest level. Even though our intention might be to find a way through the Wall, we often are tempted to try to find an easy way around it. Yet the Wall remains.

The process of going through the Wall involves learning to break through the barriers of our will and develop a deep awareness of God in our lives. The outcome is that we can allow God to be God, no strings attached. The mystery of this time is the process of psychological and spiritual healing that we undergo. It is God who is doing these things within us. We have a choice: we can either return to an earlier stage of faith, get stuck and not submit our will to God, or we can persevere through this difficult time. It is important to note that not everyone progresses to this stage. Also, some people will confront the Wall once, and others multiple times.

Table 2: Stages in the Life of Faith from 'The Critical Journey'

Stage	Characteristics	Caged
1 **The recognition of God** Faith is the discovery or recognition of God	Sense of awe, need, innocence, awareness; greater meaning in life	Feelings of worthlessness; spiritual bankruptcy; martyrdom, ignorance
2 **The life of discipleship** Faith is learning about God	Meaning comes from belonging; answers found in a leader, cause or belief system; sense of rightness, security in faith	Rigid righteousness; being *against*
3 **The productive life** Faith is working for God	Uniqueness in community; responsibility; reaching spiritual goals; valuing symbols	Self-centred or too zealous; feeling weary in serving; life as performance
4 **The journey inward** Faith as rediscovering God	Life or faith crisis; searching for direction; pursuit of integrity in relation to God; God released from constraints; apparent loss of faith	Questioning; self-assessment; immobilisation
The Wall The mystery of our will and God's face to face		Being strong willed, self-depreciating, guilt/shame ridden, intellectual, high achieving, shackled to doctrine
5 **The journey outward** Faith is surrendering to God	Renewed sense of God's acceptance, calling; concern and focus on other people's best interests; deep calm or stillness	Being out-of-touch with practical concerns; careless about important things
6 **The life of love** Faith is reflecting God	Christlike life in total obedience to God; wisdom from struggle; compassion for others; detachment from things and stress; living a life of abandonment	Separation from the world; neglect of self; apparent waste of life

Move forward	Catalysts movement	Key questions
Becoming part of a strong group; letting life take on more significance; finding a charismatic leader to follow; discovering the Way	Accepting self-worth; reducing isolation	How and when did I first recognise God?
Recognising uniqueness and contribution; identifying gifts; seeking responsibility	Taking risks; accepting gifts	When have I felt like part of a faith community?
Loss of certainty and/ or faith; personal crisis; feeling abandoned or looking for direction	Letting go of success; accepting vulnerability	Which gifts do I feel good about and want to share?
Letting go of self-centredness; accepting God's purpose for our lives; personal healing and pilgrimage; willingness to commit whatever the cost	Peace through giving up of self; new certainty in God; recognition of the cost of obedience	Has my faith fallen apart? Why?
	Tolerance of discomfort; surrender, healing, awareness, forgiveness, acceptance, love; closeness to God; discernment, solitude, reflection	
Evolving and growing deeper; seeing God in all of life; being in relationship with God	Vocation is satisfying; being whole is enough	Do I have a glimpse of God's purpose in my life?
		How is God everything to me?

THE JOURNEY OF SUFFERING AS TRANSFORMATION - IN ALLEGORY

While linear models provide us with a guide to our Christian journey through stages, allegory is a form of narrative that is used to explain difficult concepts or experiences we might come up against. This literary method has most famously been used in John Bunyan's *Pilgrim's Progress*[17], which was written in 1678 to describe the journey of the Christian life. Two more recent allegories that have explored suffering as a journey include *The Shack*[18] and *Hinds' Feet on High Places.*[19] As we read these stories, it is important to grasp the meaning they are trying to get across to us, rather than focusing on their theological accuracy, which is distracting and takes us away from the lesson they are teaching.

The Shack

The Shack explores the impact of suffering on our perception of God's goodness. It wrestles with issues such as the place of good and evil in the world, judgement, forgiveness, God's sovereignty and how this relates to grace and love.

It is a powerful story of a man named Mackenzie, 'Mack', who has suffered great emotional pain through the actions of his father, an abusive alcoholic, and the tragic abduction and murder of his younger daughter Missy. Mack blames God for the loss of his daughter. Why, if God is so powerful, did he just stand back and not intervene to save her?

---

17 Bunyan, *The Pilgrim's Progress*.
18 Young, Jacobsen & Cummings, *The Shack*.
19 Hurnard, *Hinds' Feet on High Places*.

Filled with doubt and pain, Mack enters 'The Great Sadness', which threatens to overtake everything in his life. His relationships with his wife, older daughter, son and friends become strained and distant because his pain overwhelms everything to the point that he loses perspective.

The book explores Mack's pain through a dream, where he meets God at the shack where the murder of his child occurred. But this place of pain is not what he expected it to be. It turns out to be a place where he is immersed in the loving relationship and life of the Trinity. Through this relationship, he is taken on a journey of wrestling with his pain.

In *The Shack*, God the Father, God the Son and God the Spirit are personified. God the Father is embodied in the form of an African American mother figure called Elousia,[20] who bakes bread in the kitchen and absorbs his questions about his daughter's death. He accuses her of abandoning Missy and blames her for her death. Elousia challenges him by replying, 'when all you see is your pain you lose sight of me'. She adds that love always leaves a mark, and she reveals the scars on her arms that show her identification with the suffering of Christ in the crucifixion. She says that she never left him, or Missy or Christ in their pain, but felt it with them. She created people to be loved, and this love exists in relationship. Unresolved pain stops us from fulfilling our purpose.

The second metaphor relates to the work of the Spirit in tending and changing us – as if we were a wild garden and God is the gardener. Mack is invited to work in his garden to clear an area that is wild and filled with plants with potentially deadly roots. The

---

20   Meaning Creator God, the ground of all Being.

work is hard, and it is done in partnership with the Spirit embodied as a woman named Sarayu.[21] The task he must undertake here is to understand that God does not cause suffering, but also does not necessarily stop it either. If he trusted God, he would believe that everything works for his good. But his struggle is that it is difficult to continue to believe that God is good.

The third metaphor explores our relationship with Jesus, embodied as a Middle Eastern male carpenter. Jesus gives Mack a boat to take out on the lake alone. When his boat reaches the middle of the lake, it is overcome by a black liquid, which represents the pain that is consuming him. The boat starts to break up and threatens to sink. Jesus walks out over the lake to save him, asking Mack to simply keep his eyes on him and not the sinking boat. Jesus explains that he wants us to be family and not his slaves, so that we have free will to live in relationship with him and feel what it is like to be truly loved.

The fourth metaphor is of God embodied as Wisdom, who challenges Mack's view of judgement. It is Mack's view that God does not love his children very well and is to blame for all the pain and suffering in the world. Mack is asked to take God's place in the seat of judgement to choose whether his remaining son and daughter will go to heaven. Mack discovers that because of his great love for his children, he is unable to condemn them to hell, and instead offers himself in their place. Likewise, he is challenged to see God's great love and desire for all people to be in relationship with him, and that like Mack, this love led God to give up his son Jesus to die in their place. God's love for us cost everything. God agrees that

---

21 Meaning Wind.

Missy didn't deserve to suffer, that what happened to her was the work of evil, and that no-one is immune from evil. God invites Mack to give up being the judge and instead learn to trust him.

In the final metaphor, God the Father takes on the form of an American Indian papa figure who takes Mack back to the pain of facing Missy's death. They reclaim her body and place it in a coffin, and in the midst of relationship with the Trinity, Missy is laid to rest in the cleared space in Mack's garden. The tears he has cried over time, which were collected by Sarayu, are used to bring new life to the ground around this place, and a strong tree grows. This metaphor explores forgiveness as healing. God wants to redeem everyone. Forgiveness takes time, and it often takes the form of repeated choices to let go and forgive that get easier with time. Again, God asks us to trust him; we do not have to take this journey alone. For Mack, the end of this process transformed The Great Sadness into a Profound Sense of Joy. His pain was externalised, re-storied and transformed.

Hinds' Feet on High Places

In a second allegory, *Hinds' Feet on High Places*,[22] Hannah Hurnard provides an important female perspective on the process of finding faith and then entering life as a follower of Christ the Shepherd. Her writing is shaped by her own personal story of faith and work as a missionary in the Middle East. She wrote this book over a three-week period while she was staying in Switzerland on holiday after having returned to the United Kingdom for a short period due to the death of her father.[23]

---

22   Hurnard, *Hinds' Feet on High Places*.
23   Ibid., p. 245.

This allegory looks at the fears we face through our life, and the invitation of Christ to embrace suffering and sorrow as a way to grow and be transformed into people that are more like him. The story is based on Habakkuk 3:19, 'The Sovereign LORD is my strength; he makes my feet like the feet of a deer, he enables me to tread on the heights.'

Before reading further, I challenge you to search the internet for images of hinds' feet, and you will get a clear sense of where this allegory is taking you. It is completely amazing to me that mountain goats can even climb sheer cliff faces.

In this story, the main character Much Afraid lived in the Valley of Humiliation, in a family of Fearings. Wanting to escape, she is invited by the Shephard to trust him and leave the Valley for the High Places. He offers to take her there himself, into the borderland of his Father's Kingdom, the Realm of Love. His promise is that although the journey will be difficult, he will go with her and give her hinds' feet[24] like his own so that she can climb the mountains safely. He promises her that this is possible, and that he will heal her lame and malformed feet, and her ugly crooked mouth, in the mountains as she nears the High Places. To enter the Kingdom of Love, she will need to be changed completely and will be given a new name. This is an invitation to follow and surrender completely to the way of the Shepherd. The path of faith is one of repeated invitations to surrender her will.

To assist her on her journey, Much Afraid is given two handmaidens, Suffering and Sorrow, to accompany her as her teachers. She is instructed to hold their hands and accept their

---

24   Feet of a mountain goat/deer.

help. At times she resists this and does not want their help, and when she does so the struggle creates more pain. She learns instead to accept their help. On her journey, she faces difficulties such as fear, loneliness, disappointment, frustration, loss and doubt. The four key lessons she learns are:

- to accept what happens in life with joy
- bear all that other people do against her and to forgive them
- the Shepherd sees her not as she is but as the person she will become, and he does so with grace and love
- every circumstance in life – if reacted to with love, forgiveness and obedience to God's will – can be transformed.[25]

When she arrives in the High Places, Much Afraid is healed by the Shepherd and given a new name, Grace and Glory. The two handmaidens she was given as companions were similarly transformed into Peace and Joy. She also finds that her capacity to love is transformed from a longing to be loved by other people to a godly, unconditional love that can be freely given to others.

At the end of her journey, she reflects on what she has learned through this long and painful process:

Therefore I begin to think, my Lord, you purposely allow us to be brought into contact with the bad and the evil things that you want changed. Perhaps that is the very reason why we are here in this world, where sin and sorrow and suffering and evil abound, so that we may let you teach us so to react to them, that out of them we create lovely qualities to live forever. This is the only really satisfactory way of dealing with evil, not simply binding it so that it cannot work harm, but whenever possible overcoming it with good.[26]

---

25 Hurnard, *Hinds' Feet on High Places*, pp. 229–230.
26 Ibid., pp. 230–231.

SUMMARY

Whether presented as a model with stages of growth or as a journey of transformation through allegory, these ideas open up new ways of making sense of our story of faith and the process of struggling through suffering. The thinking of those who have gone before us offers us insights into how we can progress down this difficult road and not get stuck. They direct our paths and offer solidarity in our experience. They externalise our problems, and they call us to have courage and persevere as we venture into the unknown. To be willing to go even deeper into our faith and relationship with God until we get to the point where our will is surrendered in the deepest possible way. We come face to face with God and ourselves, and we are faced with a choice about which way we want to venture. There is no quick and painless way through suffering. It is a process that we join together with God to undertake – one that is full of mystery and outside of our human control. A new direction, new life and new narrative come out of this period of darkness and sorrow, The Wall, The Great Sadness, and fear.

If I am honest, parts of each of these models and allegories ring true in my life journey. I have felt darkness and despair, been stuck in front of an impossible wall, struggling to understand God in my great sadness, and feeling afraid and overwhelmed by the problems I have faced. It is these pieces of literature, together with the words of songs, and the sharing of stories with my friends, that have helped me look beyond my own thoughts and feelings and instead see my situation through God's eyes. He has worked in me when I was too weak to do anything. I have found beyond all things, 'the shadow proves the sunshine.'[27]

JOSHUA: YOUTH STRUGGLING WITH FAITH

'Oh My God' by Jars of Clay[28] is a song that talks about how all people are suffering and their response is to call to God for help, but the best thing is the song lists all types of people who do this – respected and despised people. Suffering made me feel lonely, and this song helped me know I was not alone. We need a way to communicate and go through these things together.

KIM: HAVING A SAME SEX-ATTRACTED CHILD

Books have been helpful because they provided me with a lived example of someone going through a similar journey. I found a pastor who was safe to process this issue with.

27   Foreman, J.M. 'The Shadow Proves the Sunshine', *Nothing is Sound*, Switchfoot, C/B/O Apra Amcos, 2005.
28   Mason, S., Haseltine, D. & Lowell, C. 'Oh My God', *Good Monsters*, Jars of Clay, Universal Music, 2006.

PHOEBE: PARENTING A CHILD WITH A SEVERE MENTAL ILLNESS

I was encouraged by Parker Palmer's book *Your Life as Vocation*, about his journey through depression, doors opening and closing, and God holding you. I read Tim Costello's books about how to live out your life as a disciple of Christ, and I identified with Henry Nouwen's concept of solitude versus loneliness.

RICHARD: DEATH OF A GRANDCHILD

My granddaughter's favourite song was '10,000 Reasons'. The last verse talks about when life is coming to an end and our strength is failing, that we will still sing God's praise forever. We sang it at the funeral.[29]

29   Redmann, M & Myrin, J. '10,000 Reasons (Bless the Lord)', *10,000 Reasons*, Shout Publishing, 2011.

ENGAGING IN THE DISCIPLINE OF SUFFERING: MAKING SENSE OF FAITH AND SUFFERING

Exercise 1: Which part of these texts do you relate to?

- Which name do you most identify with as a description of your suffering?
  - The Dark Night of the Spirit
  - Suffering and Sorrow
  - The Wall
  - The Great Sadness
- Which of the two linear models of growth resonates with you? Why?
- What do you think might be caging you at the Wall? Can you see a catalyst of change that might help you move past this place?

Exercise 2: Read one of the texts

Commit to reading through one of the books that have been outlined in this chapter:

- *Dark Night of the Soul*
- *The Critical Journey*
- *The Shack*
- *Hinds' Feet on High Places*

Allow God to teach you something through your learning. Be open to what the Spirit says to you while you do this.

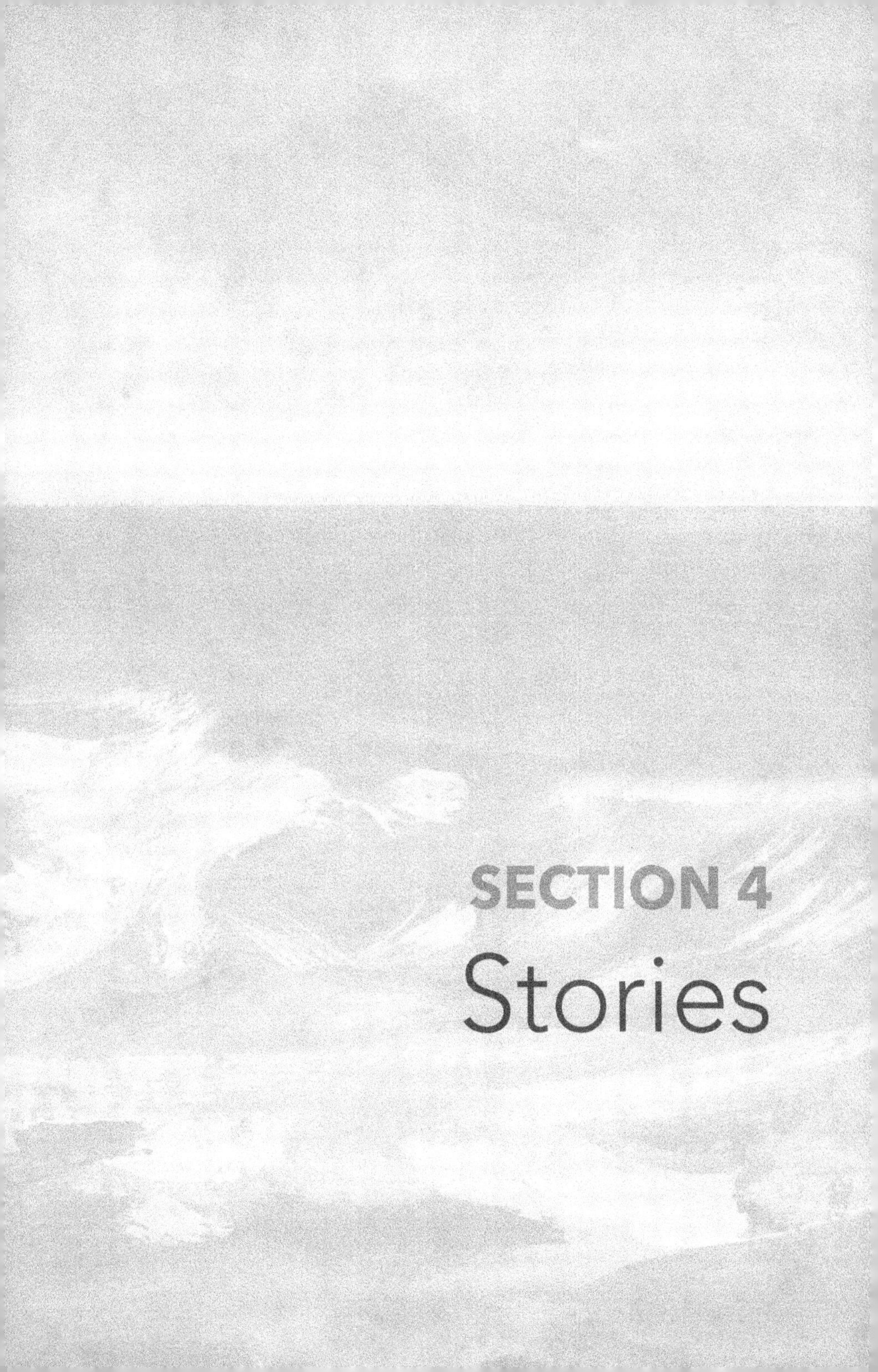

SECTION 4
Stories

10
The Small Stories We Tell Ourselves

Earlier I related a story of when someone phoned me up and said something painful to me after my brother died. I actually cannot remember what they said now, but the conversation left an indelible mark. I thought that it would have been better if I had died, and not my brother. This was both very painful and powerful. If I am honest, when these thoughts came through my head, I fully believed them – one hundred per cent. It took weeks and months of processing my grief before I could get some distance from my thoughts and see they were not true. I am sure that you have your own version of a painful thought that plagues and paralyses you. In this chapter, we are going to take a look at these thoughts and explore ways of taking the pain out of their sting.

The small stories that are generated by our rational thoughts can be formidable. In a 24-hour period, we can have as many as 70,000 thoughts.[1] Most of the time, they flow through our head in a constant stream of dialogue that we are not really aware of.

---

1 Johnstone, *Quiet the Mind*, p. 14.

Many will be positive or neutral. It is the problematic ones that cause us grief, because they can be so intense and compelling that they shape and define us in the direction of fear, apathy, despair, discouragement and helplessness.

English entertainer Derren Brown has illustrated the power our thoughts can have on our life. In one of his performances, he invited a woman to come up on stage, sit at a table and watch him eat a piece of glass. He then invited her to do the same thing, carefully breaking down the problem into little manageable steps and talking her through the process slowly. To the surprise of the audience, she was able to pick up, chew and swallow the glass without any harm to herself. There were no gimmicks. The performance was completely real. Brown was able to get an ordinary person to do something they had never done before by changing the story in their head. In this case, the story was that 'glass is dangerous and you must not touch it because it will cut you.' This internal script was transformed so that it said something like, 'glass is dangerous, but you can swallow it if you are very careful and learn to do this safely, step-by-step.'

This is an example of how powerful stories are. One of our biggest problems is that we mindlessly act on all sorts of stories all through the day, and they influence the choices we make, how we feel about ourselves and who we think God is. We rarely stop to think about whether the stories are helpful, accurate or true.

This situation is compounded further when we experience a problem that causes great pain and suffering, because it is a human response for our mind to fill up with stories that are specific to what we are going through. In fact, the painful story can become so loud in our head that it excludes all other thoughts and warps our perspective. This is never healthy or helpful. As with what happened to me when my brother died, we are vulnerable to becoming a victim of their power.

To better understand the power of story and how thoughts define who we are and how we act, we need to delve into behaviour science and psychological theory. One approach to the impact of words and story on our thinking, feelings and behaviour can be found in functional contextualism and a theory that stems from this, called relational frame theory. These psychological approaches emphasise that the context of our thoughts actually matters, and it can provide us with insight into why we think what we do and how we can change our response to our thoughts in a positive way.

FUNCTIONAL CONTEXTUALISM

Functional contextualism recognises that our behaviour is shaped by our social and physical environment, historically and in the present.[2] It states that it is essentially meaningless to examine our behaviour outside of our context because it shapes the function of our behaviour. So, even though two behaviours might look identical, their function can be very different according to the context in which they occur.

Functional contextualism allows us to form theories about why our thoughts and behaviours occur, so that we can intervene and change them.[3] It tries to accurately predict and influence our

---

2   Boone et al., 'Acceptance and Commitment Therapy'; Vilardaga, Hayes & Schelin, 'Philosophical, Theoretical and Empirical Foundations of Acceptance and Commitment Therapy'; Hayes, Barnes-Holmes & Wilson, 'Contextual Behavioural Science'.
3   Herbert & Padovani, 'Contextualism, Psychological Science, and the Question of Ontology'.

psychological interactions.[4] It judges the usefulness and the *truth* of a particular thought or behaviour according to whether it moves us towards a given goal and is consistent with our values. This is called the *pragmatic truth criterion*. In a Christian context, the pragmatic truth criterion can help us decide whether our thoughts and behaviours are moving us toward being Christlike and if they are consistent with our values that define who we want to be. This principle is shown in Figure 1. Our choice about whether to accept or reject the truth of our thoughts is influenced by a number of factors including our faith, culture and family.[5]

From this perspective, it is the context in which unhelpful thoughts occur that determines their consequences.[6] So when my thought that it would have been better if I had died occurred shortly after my brother's death, it was understandable. But when the thought came in at a different time and in a different context, it was extremely unhelpful. It was also untrue, because it did not make sense in light of my faith in God. God would not will this. And it was potentially destructive, because it led me to a very dark place in my thinking.

So, we need to identify the presence of the lingering pattern of destructive thoughts that might have inadvertently arisen from or even created our suffering and pain. When we believe our thoughts, we need to ask ourselves 'Where does it take you? Is that where you want to be?'[7] Placed in the context of our faith, we need to ask whether it is towards Christlikeness.

---

4 Vilardaga, Hayes & Schelin, 'Philosophical, Theoretical and Empirical Foundations of Acceptance and Commitment Therapy'; Hayes, Barnes-Holmes & Wilson, 'Contextual Behavioural Science'.
5 Boone et al., 'Acceptance and Commitment Therapy', p. 645.
6 Ciarrochi, Rob & Godsell, 'Letting a Little Nonverbal Air into the Room', p. 83.
7 Ibid., p. 83.

Behaviour	
What away behaviours (like running) do you do?	What toward behaviours (like hug) could you do?
Away from Christ	**Toward Christ**
What unwanted internal stuff (like fear) shows up in you?	Who and what's important?
Thoughts	

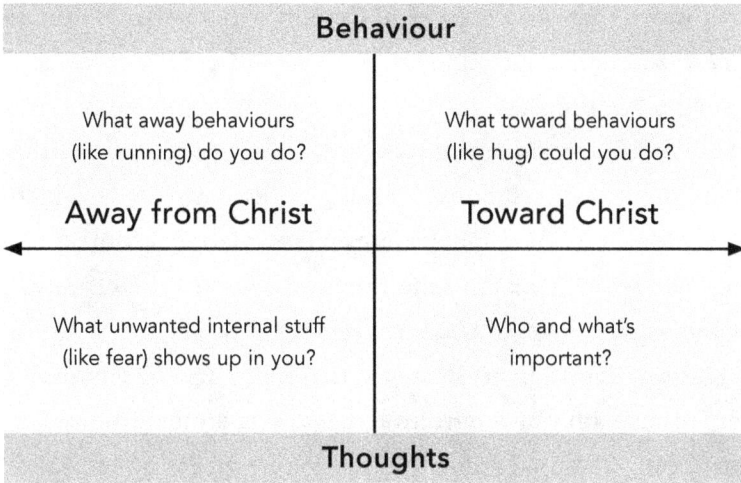

Figure 1: The pragmatic truth criterion in a Christian context[8]

In order to delve deeper into understanding whether our thoughts and behaviour are contributing to becoming Christlike, we need to go to the core of our human thoughts and language. This is why relational frame theory developed out of functional contextualism.

RELATIONAL FRAME THEORY

According to relational frame theory, our language and thoughts come from learning to relate events not simply on the basis of their formal properties (e.g. size, shape) but also on the basis of arbitrary cues. This means that context matters. The example that is commonly used to illustrate this point is that small children value coins according to their size, but as they get older, they start to recognise that the actual value of the coin is more important than the physical size.[9] For example, in Australia, a $2 coin is

---

8 Polk, 'The ACT Matrix'.
9 Hayes, 'Acceptance and Commitment Therapy', p. 874

worth more than a $1 coin even though it is smaller. These *relational frames* begin early in life when we are children developing language. We then use these relational frames to interpret and understand the world around us.

This process of relational framing is regulated by two factors: the relational and functional context. The relational context determines what you think, and the functional context determines the psychological impact of what you think.[10]

Relational frames are learned through life experiences and interactions with our environment. So, it is almost impossible to control our relational context in order to prevent unhelpful relations from being formed. For most of us, we have developed some variation of the relational frame that we are 'stupid', 'bad' or 'lazy'. Once we have formed this relation, it can be inhibited (e.g. we push it out of our mind, or we challenge it as being irrational or unhelpful) but we cannot fully unlearn it. We do, however, have some control over the functional context. We can use skills based on relational frame theory to reduce the automatic and unhelpful control these thoughts have on us.[11] Therefore, it is not the accuracy or believability of the thought that is important; rather, it is possible to allow the thought to remain there and experience it in a way that does not negatively affect your actions.[12] It is also possible to change a belief into merely a thought, without attempting to change its form – in effect, it just loses part of its power over us.

We build relationships between words, events and meanings in our mind, and these relationships work both ways. To start with, the

---

10   Ibid., p. 875.
11   Ibid.
12   Twohig, 'Introduction', p. 501.

relationship between things might be taught, but humans have the capacity to derive multiple other relationships through language even without further experience. We start doing this from 18 months of age.[13] Importantly, the overall 'percentage of our thoughts, images and sensations that are based on direct experience can be quite small compared to the percentage that are derived.'[14] We tend to short cut our responses to things by generalising based on our derived relations rather than responding to each direct experience on an individual basis. Sometimes this will mean that we pay more attention to the language-based rules in our head than the world around us, and as a result we become inflexible and rigid in our response.

Relational frame theory holds that because the verbal community reinforces so many instances of relating, relating itself becomes a generalized operant (or habitual way of responding) by a rather early age. Eventually, we automatically relationally frame all kinds of experiences. Anything that 'shows up', whether inside or outside our skin, is something for us to relate to something else because that is what our history has taught us to do. We soon develop huge numbers of relational networks which are further developed and refined throughout our lives.[15]

So, it is possible to accept that some of the relational frames we have built are unhelpful to us, and we can work within the functional context to change the psychological impact they have on us. This is great news for those of us who struggle with destructive and sometimes painful thoughts in our head. These thoughts come about because of hurtful things people have said to us or bad experiences that have created patterns of thinking that are toxic.

---

13 Ciarrochi, Rob & Godsell, 'Letting a Little Nonverbal Air into the Room', p. 83.
14 Ibid., p. 85.
15 Ibid., p. 86.

What is less emphasised with relational frame theory, but which is still helpful to identify, is that we can also work to create new relational frames by intentionally learning something new within a specific context. The example in Figure 2 shows how we can draw the relational frame associated with learning that you can eat glass. We learn through multiple examples about how to respond to situations. If our first experience with glass is that it 'cuts', then we will avoid touching it at all. If we see someone else eat the glass safely, our script in our mind starts to change. When we eat the glass with an apple and swallow it safely, then the relations between things in our mind change further, so that it is possible to accept that glass is safe to eat.

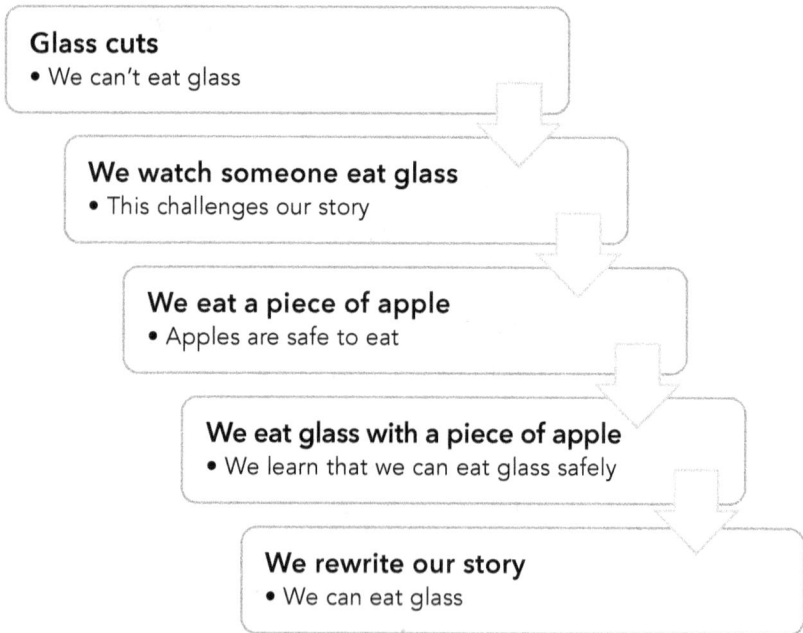

Glass cuts
• We can't eat glass

We watch someone eat glass
• This challenges our story

We eat a piece of apple
• Apples are safe to eat

We eat glass with a piece of apple
• We learn that we can eat glass safely

We rewrite our story
• We can eat glass

Figure 2: Flow of ideas that form the relational frame for eating glass

If we apply this thinking to our faith, we have two options for how we can influence our relational frames.

• We can measure our thoughts against what God says, intentionally take the power out of the unhelpful ones, and choose to act in a Christlike way rather than being destructive.

• We can intentionally learn new things to create new thoughts and stories in our head – for example, we can memorise Scripture, sing songs and be thankful to God.

This is incredibly helpful, because it provides a key to transforming our thoughts and changing our behaviour. As with any psychological tool or therapy, when we keep doing this repeatedly over time, we create new neural pathways that become more automatic. Ultimately, this process results in us changing our mind.

Before we explore these two ways of changing our relational frames, we need to recognise that our thoughts cannot be transformed through control or avoidance. Instead, our ultimate goal is to be a flexible thinker who can make healthy choices based on our values regardless of the thoughts that pop into our minds. Let's explore this idea in more detail.

THE PROBLEM OF RULE-GOVERNED BEHAVIOUR

When our stories are hurtful and harmful to us, we often engage in a struggle of control and attempt to suppress our thoughts and feelings. Research has shown that this does not work, as the thoughts and feelings do not get easier to manage but rather become stronger in our minds.[16] A common way of understanding

---

16   Stoddard & Fari, *The Big Book of ACT Metaphors*, p. 6.

this concept is through the exercise, 'Don't Think About a Puppy', which asks people to specifically not think about something. When we try this, we find that controlling our thoughts is futile as they actually come back stronger in our thinking.[17] Our mind becomes full of dogs, puppies and other baby animals. So, control does not work and only feeds further into our suffering. Our thoughts and feelings become more rigid and inflexible, and they can make our life purposeless and out of step with our values. To get to this point, we will have done at least one of the following three things:

- avoided unpleasant thoughts
- run away from and avoided our problems
- lived a life that is not consistent with our values and has no purpose.

To create meaning in the midst of these painful thoughts, we have to turn each of these behaviours the opposite way. We need to choose to

- learn to sit with and graciously accept the painful thoughts
- willingly face our problems
- clarify and live consistently with our values, and find purpose in our faith.

There is a practical application of the concepts found in functional contextualism and relational frame theory that makes it possible to create meaning despite painful thoughts. It is known as Acceptance and Commitment Therapy (ACT).[18] This therapy employs the techniques of metaphor and cognitive distancing to make us more aware of the thoughts that flow through our mind, to accept them and to discern which ones are going to be helpful

---

17 Ibid., p. 36.
18 A postmodern variation of cognitive behavioural therapy.

to act on. The strength of this approach is that it readily integrates our faith into this process because the way we evaluate a thought is based on our values. It gives practical direction to assist us in evaluating whether a particular thought or behaviour is healthy or *true*, and whether it is moving us towards being more like Christ. It does this by confronting and disputing our thoughts using metaphors. These word pictures challenge the relational frames in our mind, together with our *truth*, in a uniquely powerful and transformative way.

METAPHORS

Language can be used to form metaphors that create a verbal world where we can explore new behaviours and discover new alternatives to our restricted relational frames. Examples include

- the *Great Storyteller*, a metaphor used to illustrate the way our thoughts come through our mind in a never-ending narrative that is full of judgements, rules and memories[19]

- the *Tug-Of-War*, a metaphor used to describe our attempts to control our thoughts – the more we try to control them, the stronger they become and the more effort we need to exert to distract ourselves from them or push them away

- *Feeding the Tiger*, which speaks to our tendency to maintain a problem the more we think about it and give energy to it; it becomes bigger over time.[20]

When the right one is applied, these metaphors can change our relational frames. This is why Jesus spoke in parables (i.e. stories that illustrate a moral or spiritual lesson) – they stretch our thinking about God and ourselves. For example, in the parable of the

---

19 Harris, *The Happiness Trap.*
20 Forsyth & Eifert, *The Mindfulness and Acceptance Workbook for Anxiety.*

two builders, he explained how his values and Way would provide us with a solid foundation on which to build our life.

Now that we have a foundational understanding of how to approach our painful thoughts, we will apply this to two practical techniques that can put this into action in our lives. The first is cognitive distancing, which helps us step back from our unhelpful thoughts to reflect on their *truth* and whether to act on them. The second uses thankfulness to intentionally develop positive healthy relational frames.

COGNITIVE DISTANCING

The first way we can challenge our relational frame is by learning to create distance from our thoughts. When we totally believe a thought is *true*, we can get stuck or *fused* to it.[21] We lose the ability to get the perspective we need to work out whether our belief is correct or even helpful. For example, if I think it would be better if I was dead rather than my brother, I could fully believe this is true and fuse myself to it, like literally sticking to it like glue, or I could step back, see the thought as a story about my grief, get some perspective, and challenge whether this thought is appropriate in my current context without pushing it away.[22] I can then see my thought less literally and realise it is not necessary *true*. It is just a thought.

This process of stepping back from your thoughts so that they are less powerful is called *cognitive distancing*, or *defusion*. It recognises that we do not have to totally believe and buy into everything we think. We can get distance from our thoughts by just noticing

---

21   Boone et al., 'Acceptance and Commitment Therapy', p. 648.
22   Ciarrochi, Rob & Godsell, 'Letting a Little Nonverbal Air into the Room', p. 89.

them, giving them a name and thanking our mind for them, or repeating the thought over and over for 30 seconds until it is a meaningless collection of sounds. These simple techniques take the power out of the word or story to provide us with enough objectivity to question their helpfulness and then choose to focus on something that is more worthwhile and meaningful.

For followers of Christ, we might not be able to delete unhelpful thoughts but we can change how we respond to them, because as a new creation in Christ we have a new context and a renewed mind (2 Cor 5:11, Rom 12:2). Experiencing true freedom in Christ means we will not be trapped by our old relational frames. We will instead choose to respond to our thoughts in light of the good news of Christ and how God sees us and the world.

FOSTERING THANKFULNESS

The second way we can change our relational frames is to intentionally create new ones. Positive psychology[23] has reminded us that gratitude is a powerful tool for changing our outlook on the world. It is not a new concept. In the Old and New Testaments, and in church tradition, we have practised the disciplines of worship and thanksgiving for hundreds of years. But gratitude is more than just these things. It is about adopting an attitude to life that is God and other focused, which intentionally concentrates on things that are life giving and edifying. This creates positive relational frames and patterns of thinking.

When the Old Testament talks about meditating on Scripture (Josh 1:8), it means more than just reading it. It involves taking

---

23   See Seligman, *Flourish.*

the words into our inmost being so that we live and breathe them throughout our day. This is how we can positively impact our thinking and choose to change it by learning to see the world through God's eyes.

In Philippians 4:8 it says, 'whatever is true, whatever is noble, whatever is right, whatever is pure, whatever is lovely, whatever is admirable – if anything is excellent or praiseworthy – think about such things.' If we do this, we change what feeds our minds. Even the simple discipline of gratitude and thankfulness to God changes our thoughts so that they are positive and edifying rather than just focused on problems, failures and shortcomings.

TOWARDS TRANSFORMING OUR STORIES

The hope that both functional contextualism and relational frame theory provide is a practical path forward to change the impact of our painful stories so that they are no longer so problematic in our daily lives. It also opens up possibilities to create new patterns of thinking that are healthy and transform our lives in a positive way. The overarching principle that we are directed by is whether our thoughts and behaviours are moving us closer to being like Christ in our character and actions. We have a measuring stick to use in our evaluation, something we can anchor our *truth* to.

We can use our newly gained skills to learn to eat glass if we want to, but I think that perhaps a better thing to learn is how to be more aware of our thoughts so that we can gain some perspective and distance from them when they are unhelpful; be gracious and accept pain when it comes; and pursue our values despite what life throws at us. These habits will take us deeper into the process of psychological and spiritual transformation.

When I think about my thought that I should have died and not my brother, I know this is not true. It still comes into my head when I am discouraged, but I now see it for what it is – a lie. It has no power over me anymore. My brother's favourite Bible passage was Romans 8:38–39, and it reminds me that nothing can separate me from God's love. This is all that matters, and it is enough to completely undermine the power of the painful memory I carry.

BROOKE: ABANDONMENT IN MARRIAGE

I need to be strong for my kids because they are hurting. He walked out on all of us.

JAMES: PARENT OF A CHILD WITH A SEVERE DISABILITY

How are we going to connect with other people? My burden can't be shared with others because it is too hard to explain or have others enter into it. I can't share pain with others and pretend in front of other people that things are ok. Withdrawal is a temptation. All we do is survive and get through each day. My son's story is irrelevant to ministry. It is not engaging to people, because it is so far outside of most people's experience. They can't understand.

KARLY: MINISTRY LOSS

It's not fair. What can I do to make it right? I'm so glad my husband's parents are dead [and don't know about what's happened]. I used to fantasise about what I could do – for example, confront the person – because I didn't get a chance to say what I thought. These thoughts were more a release of frustration. I never acted on them.

KIM: HAVING A SAME SEX-ATTRACTED CHILD

Why hadn't we picked this up sooner? How are we going to deal with this in our wider family? This has implications for my husband's work. What is going to happen next?

MICHAEL: MINISTRY BURNOUT

I'm wrong. It's my fault. I'm a bad minister, a bad leader. I'm responsible. I questioned my identity as a follower of Christ and didn't know if my faith would survive. My thoughts were about the fear of rejection.

RICHARD: DEATH OF A GRANDCHILD

I'll never see her being married. She'll never have a 21st birthday. Why? I dreamed about what could have been.

PHOEBE: PARENTING A CHILD WITH A SERIOUS MENTAL ILLNESS

I used to think about my daughter – *I don't like you. You are making my life difficult. It's not fair.* But if I didn't have children, I'd be a shallow person. Relationships challenge what you think about life.

JOSHUA'S STORY: YOUTH STRUGGLING WITH FAITH

If these people call themselves Christian, is Christ someone worth following?

ENGAGING IN THE DISCIPLINE OF SUFFERING: CHANGING OUR THINKING

Exercise 1: Cognitive distancing strategies (evaluating our thoughts)

Can you identify any thoughts that really bring you down and get under your skin? Here's some general examples that might help get you started:

- 'I can't do this.'
- 'No-one likes me.'
- 'I'm stupid.'

If you have experienced a very painful period in your life due to illness, relationship breakdown, childhood neglect or abuse, trauma, grief and loss, or mental illness, you might have some more specific thoughts. I want you to try to make a new pattern of response to these thoughts so that they are not as powerful in your mind.

1. Create distance
For example,

- recognise that what you are thinking is just a thought
- try giving the thought a pet name
- say it out loud
- repeat it over and over until it sounds like meaningless noise.

2. Measure the thought against the Bible and how God sees you
Ask yourself the following questions:

- If Christ was next to you, what would he say about the truth of this thought?
- What does the Bible say about how God sees you?

3. Surrender your thought to God

Pray and talk to God about it. Metaphorically lay it at God's feet, and let it go.

4. Refocus your mind on something that is meaningful

Examples include

- doing your work
- spending time with a friend
- going for a walk.

Exercise 2: Intentionally making positive thought patterns

- At the end of each day, take the time to thank God for the things you are grateful for.
- Reflect on what you feed your mind with during the day. How does this measure against God's values? What is one thing that you could change so that your thinking pattern is more godly?
- Make a commitment to consistently read the Bible each day and try to apply it to your life with the help of the Holy Spirit.

11
The Spiritual Discipline of Story Changing

I recently went through a time of transition in both my work roles and ministry focus. I felt God tell me to specifically leave one financially secure job and step out and do something different. The only problem was that I did not know what that *different* was supposed to be. In mid-2019, I left my job with only a sketchy idea of what the future was meant to look like and started to work one hundred per cent of the time for myself, trusting God to provide enough money to live on.

At the end of 2019, my friends in my Bible study group were discussing Luke 5:1–11, where Jesus challenges Simon the fisherman to put his boat out into the deep water and let down the nets for a catch. As a group, we asked God to speak to us through the passage and spent time contemplating the words silently as individuals. We then came back together to share what we thought the Spirit was saying to us. One of the things we shared was how God sees ahead, and how he knows. He is Jehovah Jireh, the God who sees. Jesus knew that the disciples would catch so many fish that their nets would begin to break and the boats would start to sink.

Unbeknown to them, I had been pondering this passage for some weeks, knowing that God was telling me to let down my nets again. I felt led by the Spirit that something was going to change, but I could not see what or how. The discussion in my Bible study group that night helped me to further clarify what God was trying to teach me. I was reassured that he knew what was ahead, even when it was hidden from me, because he is the God who sees.

In the example I've used here from my own life, some important things came together to change my mind and challenge my thinking. I had been meditating on Jesus' teaching through my own discipline and practice of reading Scripture, and I had shared my journey with other Christians. Through these things, the Spirit was speaking to me, and it was the image of letting down nets that was central to what I was needing to learn, which in turn had implications for how I understood God.

THE LIFE-CHANGING POWER OF JESUS' TEACHING

Jesus recognised that language – the use of metaphor, parables, images and names – was an essential part of teaching and transforming people's lives. When we think about it, he spent a great deal of his time challenging people's relational frames and helping them to see God differently. His parables had a similar purpose to the metaphors used in Acceptance and Commitment Therapy, as they pushed people to think outside their normal experience. In all these things, his *truth criterion* against which all things were measured was if they reflected the values of the kingdom of God.

James Bryan Smith[1] argues that focusing on Jesus' teaching can change the stories in our head. He recognises that we are shaped by our stories and they determine much of our behaviour. Often they are both running and ruining our lives, and this is why it is so important that the stories are correct. We need to measure our stories against those of Jesus, then go the next step of adopting Jesus' stories as our own.

In order to do this, we need to do what Jesus said in his Sermon on the Mount, and 'Repent, for the kingdom of heaven has come near' (Matt 3:2). The term used here for repent is *metanoia*, which means to change your mind and purpose. As followers of Christ, we are called to change the stories we have been given by our family, culture and world, so that we have new stories that are based on the kingdom of God. Adopting the teaching of Jesus is one way we can do this. But it cannot stop with just our head knowledge. It needs to be a combination of

- changing our thoughts, or relational frames
- living differently
- doing these things in community
- being led by the Holy Spirit.[2]

This approach will help us to address what Dallas Willard[3] has described as the shortcomings of Western evangelical Christianity. We have been so focused on accumulating head knowledge and believing in God that we have forgotten to put this together with the practical living out of our faith each day through the spiritual

---

1   Bryan Smith, *The Good and Beautiful God*, pp. 25–26.
2   Ibid., pp. 23–24.
3   See Willard, *The Spirit of the Disciplines*.

disciplines, living in community in the body of Christ, and having a deep, abiding, continuous relationship with Christ.

When we move from head knowledge to practically living out our faith, we see that the Holy Spirit is the agent of change within us that works through these parables and teachings of Christ to change our thoughts, which in turn is reflected and reinforced by our daily use of prayer, reading Scripture and silence. We then live this in community with other people who join with us in reflecting on Jesus' teaching and keeping us accountable in applying it to our lives. The result is transformation of our whole life from the inside out (see Figure 3).

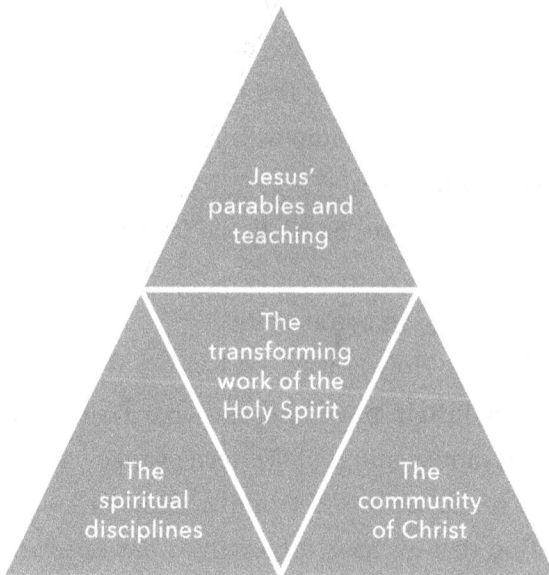

Figure 3: Adaption of James Bryan Smith's model of the four components of personal transformation.[4]

---

4   Smith, *The Good and Beautiful God*, p. 24.

We are now going to look more closely at each part of Bryan Smith's model of transformation and consider how it can help us to grapple with pain and suffering. The aim is to transform our relational frames intentionally, in partnership with the work of the Holy Spirit. We will do this through immersing ourselves in Jesus' teaching, engaging in the spiritual disciplines, being encouraged in our faith through the body of the church, and allowing the Holy Spirit to speak through all these things for change.

JESUS' PARABLES AND TEACHING

The teaching of Jesus is the first of the four components of personal transformation described in the model above. Jesus used everyday things to communicate important lessons about life, God and what his kingdom was like through parables, or simple stories. He also taught that people who listened to what he said with an attitude of openness would understand his words and stories and learn from them.

An example is the parable of the sower, where a farmer scatters seed on different soils. Only the seed sown on good soil bears fruit (Matt 13:23). The point Jesus was making was that his teaching will have no impact on our life if we immediately forget it or do not understand its meaning (Matt 13:19), if we ignore it during times of adversity (Matt 13:20–21), or if it is swallowed up by our worries about life or our chasing after money and possessions (Matt 13:22).

Jesus reinforces this point on one of his visits to the house of Mary and Martha. Martha was distracted and busy performing the socially appropriate role of offering hospitality to her guests, while her sister Mary had stopped to sit at Jesus' feet and listen to him. After Martha complained to Jesus that Mary wasn't helping her, he replied that Mary had chosen the better path (Luke 10:38–42). Likewise, we need to get better at stopping, being still and spending time immersing ourselves in the person of Jesus.

The question we could ask is, how can we possibly be still and stop and have an open attitude when our suffering closes our mind so that all it thinks about is The Problem? Thankfully, Jesus offers us some helpful metaphors to keep our eyes focused on the right things so that we do not ruminate about our problems or the past. Through these stories, he encourages us to keep our focus on what we can control, by living each day in a way that is consistent with his teachings, life and example. He encourages us to let go of the past, focus on today and not fret about the future. In other words, live fully in the present.

Letting go of the past

Ploughing a field

When a farmer ploughs a field, the only way they can make the furrows regular and even is by focusing on something ahead of them, keeping their gaze forward. Jesus uses this image to teach us about the attitude we need to have if we want to live for the kingdom of God (Luke 9:62). We need to keep our eyes on Christ, and on God, so that our lives do not go off track. A straight furrow is the best kind.

Slaves

Jesus says we cannot serve both God and money (Luke 16:13), nor can we live for both God and ourselves. We must make a choice. He says that 'everyone who sins is a slave to sin. Now a slave has no permanent place in the family, but a son belongs to it forever. So if the Son sets you free, you will be free indeed' (John 8:34–36).

Focusing on today

Building a tower or a house

To build a tower, a person needs to sit down and plan the process and estimate the cost. Otherwise, how can you budget in order to successfully complete the building project? And what is the point of laying a foundation and not finishing the building? Jesus is warning us that if we want to follow him, we must really think through what we are doing and be prepared to follow despite the cost (Luke 14:28–33) – to the point where we are willing to give up all our possessions (Luke 14: 33). He says that it is not enough to just know him; we must also do what he tells us and act on his teachings every day (Luke 6:46–49). This is like the wise man who built his house on a secure foundation of rock. When a flood came, his house was not destroyed (Matt 7:24–27).

Carrying our cross daily

In Luke 9:23, Jesus says that if we want to be his disciple, we need to deny ourselves and take up our cross daily to follow him (Luke 9:23). The image of cross bearing prompts us to think of the image of Jesus carrying his cross by himself to Golgotha, where he was to be crucified (John 19:17). This image reminds us of Jesus' sacrifice for us in dying on the cross to take on our sin, how he identified with our suffering, and his resurrection that gives us new life. In the same way, we are to give up our self, our life, our control, our will, and take up Jesus' way of life each day.

The yoke

Jesus offers us an invitation to come to him if we are weary or burdened (Matt 11:28–30). He promises us rest: 'Take my yoke upon you and learn from me, for I am gentle and humble in heart, and you will find rest for your souls' (Matt 11:29).

A yoke is a wooden frame that joins work animals together to pull heavy loads. The yoke was a metaphor commonly used in Judaism to refer to the law, so in this context, discipleship meant learning from Scripture together with the additional layers of pharisaic oral law. The word was also used to describe the burden Israel felt under foreign oppression in the Old Testament (Lam 5:5). So what Jesus is saying is that being his discipline means that we are free from the law and the oppression of living for ourselves (e.g. sin), but he does not promise no burden. Rather, he will help us carry a yoke of discipleship, walking together with us and providing us with a deep existential peace as we do so.

Not fretting about the future

Storms

Sometimes our life can feel like we are in a boat sailing through a storm that is battering us. Both the waves and the wind are against us, and we worry that we will not make it to our destination. Matthew 14:22–33 describes a moment when the disciples, travelling in a boat across the Sea of Galilee during a storm, saw Jesus walking on water toward them. His words to them, 'Don't be afraid' (Matt 14:27), reassure us that he is able walk over the threatening waves of our own situations and help us in our need. And like Peter, if we dare to walk on the water ourselves but focus on the wind and waves, we are likely to be overcome with fear and sink (Matt 14:28–29). But Jesus reaches out to us to catch us and save us. He says, 'why did you doubt?' (Matt 14:31). Once again, we are urged to keep our eyes on Christ and not the problems that surround us.

Birds, grass and flowers

Jesus tells us not to spend our time worrying about material possessions (Matt 6:25–34). After all, life is not just about food or clothes. God will care for us just as he cares for the birds of the air, and the grass and flowers of the field. Even more so, as we are 'more valuable than they' (Matt 6:26). As followers of Christ, we are called to strive first for the kingdom of God and have faith that our physical needs will be met. God knows what our needs are. Jesus says, 'do not worry' (Matt 6:25).

The good shepherd

Jesus described himself as the good shepherd (John 10:11), in contrast to a hired hand who doesn't care about the sheep. When a threat comes, in the form of a wolf, the hired hand runs away. The vulnerable sheep scatter in terror, in danger of being killed. The good shepherd is not like this. He knows each of his sheep individually and they know him. If a threat comes, he will protect them and lead them to safety. If necessary, he will lay down his life to protect them from the wolf.

Likewise, as our good shepherd, Jesus knows us. And as his sheep, we know him – the one who gave his life for us. We can rely on him, trust him, listen to him and follow him to where he is leading us. He protects us, and he gives us abundant life. Jesus' metaphor of himself as a shepherd reminds us of the image of the Lord as our shepherd in Psalm 23.

All these metaphors that Jesus uses in his teaching are aimed at shifting our thinking so we can embrace an attitude of learning and openness to him, which is central to our imitation of his life.

THE SPIRITUAL DISCIPLINES

The spiritual disciplines form the second component of the model of personal transformation depicted in Figure 3.

I wonder how the word 'discipline' is heard by you. We often associate it with negative things, like chores, duties, work, and tedious but necessary tasks. Or worse still, the word takes us back to being children who are in trouble for doing something wrong. However, this is the opposite of what 'spiritual disciplines' are about. They are actually habits and practices that are designed to build character. They have been in use for hundreds of years and are based on the life and teachings of Jesus Christ. They are life-giving ways we can connect to God and maintain a relationship with him that is continuous and loving.

In this book we have been exploring the discipline of suffering, which is just one of many disciplines required for our personal transformation. Such change requires a deep, abiding relationship with Christ (John 15) where our will is completely surrendered to God in an attitude of love. It is something we can learn by modelling ourselves on Christ.

Jesus likened the state of us abiding in him to the two-way relationship a branch has with its parent vine (John 15). This metaphor helps us to understand that abiding in Jesus means that we will both listen to and speak to him as a friend. Our life comes from him, and he makes it possible for us to bear fruit like 'love, joy, peace, forbearance, kindness, goodness, faithfulness, gentleness and self-control' (Gal 5:22–23). He transforms our mind. Dallas Willard describes this process as 'God … walking through one's personality with a candle, directing one's attention to things one after the other.[5] The Spirit shines a light on the things that we need to change, the thought patterns that cause problems. And, as the Spirit reminds us of all the things Jesus taught (John 14:26), we can be transformed.

We can abide in Christ and go deeper in our two-way relationship with him by speaking in a verbal or thought-based prayer, or by listening through the reading of Scripture or sitting in silent contemplation. Listening to God is by far the harder skill to learn, so it is important to set aside time to practice.

Speaking to God

Jesus encouraged us to pray and never give up through the story he told of the persistent widow, who kept hassling her town's judge for justice (Luke 18:1–8). Jesus also told us to pray for people who persecute us (Matt 5:44), to pray alone in secret so we are not trying to impress other people (Matt 6:5–15), to ask God for the things we need (Matt 7:7–11) and to have faith that God will answer our requests (Mark 11:23–26).

In other parts of the New Testament, we are encouraged to pray without ceasing (1 Thess 5:17), to pray about everything we need and be thankful (Phil 4:6) and to pray in the Spirit all the time, and for other believers (Eph 6:18).

In all these examples, the speaking to God is done with vocalised words or thoughts in our mind. It is our familiar way to communicate with other people, our family and friends, and so it is not such a jump to use a similar approach to communicate with God. It is an important part of our relationship with God, which we need to do regularly, daily, often.

---

5 Willard, *Hearing God*, p. 135.

Listening to God

Listening to God comes less naturally to us in our Western culture because we have collectively lost the habit since the Enlightenment, when rational thought became prized. This hasn't been helped by our society's fast pace and saturation with facts and information that are streamed constantly through electronic media. Moments of stillness are rare, and increasingly hard to capture in our daily lives.

It is therefore more important than ever that we cultivate the discipline of listening to God, because it encourages stillness and wellbeing through the reading of Scripture and sitting in silent contemplation.

We can listen to God through Scripture by reading casually for content, like we do a newspaper, blog or book. We can study it, using our analytical mind to search for meaning, understand the context and squeeze every drip of knowledge out of it. We can memorise it. And we can read it meditatively, so it goes deep inside us. All these methods have their place, and each can create change.

If we believe 'All Scripture is God-breathed and is useful for teaching, rebuking, correcting and training in righteousness' (2 Tim 3:16), we will set regular time aside to read what God is saying to us through this precious text. It is essentially the same as wanting to take the time to listen to our friend to really understand them. God is revealed in Scripture the same way we understand our friends through conversation.

Of all the different ways we can read Scripture, meditating on it can be the most helpful because it is like taking a long hot bath in the word of God and soaking our entire being in it. Richard Foster describes this approach as reading with your heart while inviting the Spirit of Christ to guide us.[6] It requires a willingness on our part to relinquish our need to control and manipulate the words we read, and instead submit ourselves to the transforming work of the word of God.

The most well-known way of putting this discipline into practice is through *lectio divina* (Latin for 'divine reading'), a method of reading Scripture that involves repeated reading of a passage of Scripture. The Scripture is read with an open attitude, in expectation that God will lead us and speak to us. There are four steps:

- First reading – we read with a listening spirit
- Second reading – we reflect on what we think God is saying to us
- Third reading – we pray in response to what we have heard
- Fourth reading – we contemplate what we want to carry back into our lives.

Lectio divina can be done individually or in a group. It can also be done in one sitting or repeated daily over a longer period of time.

We can also choose to listen to Christ through contemplative, or silent, prayer. Contemplative prayer is our Christian equivalent to mindfulness. It allows us to connect to God and our self in quietness, to focus on one thing, and use our five senses in the process. As we practise this discipline, our spirit becomes still. It induces the relaxation response in our body; our breathing and heart rate slow down, we gain more concentration and better regulation of our emotions. In the silent stillness it creates, we quieten our thoughts and open ourselves up to God. If you are interested in some tools to do this in your daily life, I recommend reading *Christ-Centred Mindfulness: Connection to Self and God.*[7]

---

6 Foster, *Life with God*, p. 59.
7 Thompson, *Christ-Centred Mindfulness.*

Living out these spiritual disciplines in our daily life not only transforms our character and faith but also goes deeper to changing our thoughts. This is because we are living in a two-way relationship with God that is about listening and speaking. Scripture clearly encourages us to spend time reading and praying, and to do this regularly and often. It is the example Jesus set for us on multiple occasions. And in the context of this book, these spiritual disciplines also provide us with an opportunity to process our thoughts, stories and narratives and allow them to be challenged by the Holy Spirit.

THE COMMUNITY OF CHRIST

The third component of the model focuses on living out our faith within the body of Christ. We can be tempted to think that this is too hard and inconvenient; relationships and community are messy and require effort. As Westerners influenced by our post-modern culture, we think that individual faith is valuable, but we do not need to share it with other people for it to be authentic or healthy. However, God is not as much of a fan of personal faith as what we are often tempted to think he is. We are, in fact, meant to live our faith out with other Christians within the body of Christ. We need each other to grow, learn and be challenged in our thinking. To have it corrected when it goes off track, because life together changes our stories and encourages us to live according to the teachings of Christ.

Perhaps this is one lesson that the COVID-19 lockdowns of 2020 and 2021 have taught us. We need each other. We are social beings, and if we are left alone for too long, we become withdrawn, inward focused and trapped in our own restricted thinking. This is not healthy.

To keep perspective, we need to be able to see that we are part of something bigger, that life is more than just about us. This happens as we interact with other people and see life through other lenses. We need to be flexible and open to change, and we need to continue to learn and grow as people.

God uses people to create change. He is not just at work in us as individuals; he is at work in the world. Part of our challenge is to listen and hear where he is working to create change, and to be part of it and join in with his mission. This means that we need to work with other followers of Christ. We need to discern together what we think God is doing and be a united influence on the world around us. In this way, the changing of our minds becomes a collective process, one that transforms us, the people around us, and ultimately joins in with God's purpose for our world.

THE TRANSFORMING WORK OF THE HOLY SPIRIT

The fourth and final component of the model of personal transformation is not so much something we do, but something the Holy Spirit does in our life if we regularly contemplate Jesus' teaching, engage in spiritual disciplines that allow us to abide with God, and learn with other followers in community. The transformation is possible because we have created a space for God to work in our midst in a way that is not controlled by us. The Holy Spirit has the opportunity to reach into our minds and alter our very being because we have intentionally created an environment where we are open to this happening.

I wonder if we limit the scope of God's transformation of our thoughts because we refuse to take the time to sit and learn. Our attitude is closed, instead of open. This is probably why many of us get stuck and do not feel like a new creation in Christ. We cling to our old relational frames because they seem safe and comfortable – even if they are not healthy or good for us.

A key theme that Jesus talks about is our need to relinquish our control to God. He teaches us that if we want to follow him, we need to lose our life in order to find it again (Matt 10:39). I believe this is a discipline and a choice that we face each day. Clinging to our old patterns of thinking just perpetuates our suffering. We are not free in the way that God wishes we were.

One of my favourite writers is Sarah Bessey. She uses the metaphor of sorting boxes to describe the process of working out our faith.[8] She describes this process as feeling like we are 'sitting in a mess of half-unpacked boxes',[9] where we have the hard task of sorting through our questions, wonky thinking, grief and doubt. Over time we accumulate more and more unresolved issues, and we are asked to start to sort the boxes. In the process, we leave a trail of things behind us, which eventually frees us from all the excess weight we have been carrying.

> *But every single one of those items you leave along the trail – your cynicism, your hypocrisy, your lies, your numbing techniques, your apologetics and doctrinal statements, your worldview, your pomposity, your opinions, your carefully constructed personas, your sins, your righteousness, your secrets – all of it will become filthy rags, and in the end, you will be nearly flinging them off the wagon, glad to be rid of them at last, I promise.*[10]

---

8   Bessey, *Out of Sorts*, p. 233.
9   Ibid., p. 233.
10 Ibid., p. 234.

To embark on this process can seem daunting, and it may provoke within us the same reaction we have when we realise we need to clean out our garage! Most people don't want to do it. We are guaranteed to get dirty and tired in the process, but how good is it to stand back at the end of the job and feel a sense of satisfaction that we completed it!

CHANGING OUR STORIES

So, if I think back to my problem of leaving my job and not knowing what the future would bring, I can now see with the wisdom of hindsight that God knew the path I was meant to take the whole time, even though I could not see it. He was speaking to me through the stories about Jesus, and he challenged me to let down my nets again, in a different place. This forced me to reconsider who I thought God was. My learning was enriched by the Spirit-filled words of other Christians around me. I let go of control, and I was open to what God was saying and took a risk, even though I was not sure of the outcome.

What I see now, but could not see at the time, was that God was also working in other people and leading them in new ways. In order for my path to make sense, he needed to work in their lives as well. He was bringing our paths together so that collectively we could be transformed and be used by God in his mission in this world. This book is one of the positive things that has come out of this step of faith.

BROOKE: ABANDONMENT IN MARRIAGE

My values and priorities are still the same, but I am more outspoken than I used to be. God heals the thoughts over time, and you forget the painful things.

JAMES: PARENT OF A CHILD WITH A SEVERE DISABILITY

I am more patient, sensitive to my family's needs, less vain and ambitious, and less concerned about what others think. I am compassionate. I realise that the idea 'It can't get worse' is not helpful.

JOSHUA: YOUTH STRUGGLING WITH FAITH

I have come to see real Christians as people and not authorities on God. I shouldn't judge God by his followers' actions because people make mistakes. I am aware of my own weakness of character. Unfortunately, Christians are not always known by their love for one another, even though this is how they should be (John 13:35). The beatitudes say blessed are those who cry for they will be happy. God rewards people who persevere despite the odds. My faith is now more self-driven and not dependent on others. I have struggled to form values, and now appreciate hard work, honesty, commitment, discipline, compassion and empathy. I am more other focused and want to give back to them.

KARLY: MINISTRY LOSS

My inner life is more peaceful, spiritually mature, more accepting of things, even in my emotional journey. I have a day-to-day focus versus a future focus. I hold my future lightly. The grief is still there.

KIM: HAVING A SAME SEX-ATTRACTED CHILD

I realise I was labelling people as 'other' if they were different, including the LGBTIQ community. This group of people is not as homogenous as I had assumed, and I was passing judgement from a Christian point of view and hadn't thought about it. I hope I am now more compassionate to people rejected by the church. I think about the story of the woman caught in adultery (John 8:11), where Jesus says, 'Now go and leave your life of sin.' The church claims to bring people in, but instead drives them out. I want to be a person of peace. I don't want others to assume what I believe. I want to be more careful about what I say so I don't hurt others.

MICHAEL: MINISTRY BURNOUT

I feel a greater emphasis on being part of the kingdom here and now rather than being part of the church institution. I can see this when I read about who Jesus is and what he did. I long for significance in Christ and to be part of the church that speaks truth to power rather than being part of the status quo. God uses my grief and struggles to help others. I am more willing to rest and limit my workload. I am quicker to forgive and try and listen and hear others. I value my health more than success. I am more concerned about being in the present.

PHOEBE: PARENTING A CHILD WITH A SERIOUS MENTAL ILLNESS

Jesus didn't heal everyone or give pat answers. He used healing for the bigger picture. I am inspired by the Red-Letter Christians movement that uses Jesus' words and actions as the heart of faith. I have gone deeper, and I am more rooted in a social-justice perspective. I always come back to God; separating God from the church is important because Christianity is about the central creed and needs to be tolerant and ecumenical.

RICHARD: DEATH OF A GRANDCHILD

I couldn't have gone through it without leaning on Jesus. My understanding of who Jesus is drove me to this. I have an increased sense of preciousness of my grandkids. This comes out in how I use my time. I am available to them and make every moment count.

ENGAGING IN THE DISCIPLINE OF SUFFERING: LETTING JESUS' TEACHING TRANSFORM US

Exercise 1. Red letter Christianity

Challenge yourself to live consistently with the teachings of Jesus. These teachings, and the words Jesus said, are highlighted in red in some copies of the Bible. Make a commitment to follow these words and embody them in your life.

If you are interested, you might like to investigate the Red-Letter Christians movement.[11]

Exercise 2. Living in a faith community and allowing the Spirit to speak

Make a commitment to live your life in community with other Christians so that you are accountable for your thoughts and actions. This means finding a place where you can be authentic, where you do not have to live with a facade that covers your pain. This is especially important when you are struggling and trying to make sense of your faith and life. There are a number of ways I have connected to people and God through difficult times. This has been essential to my health and wellbeing, as well as the growth of my faith.

Here are some suggestions for you to try:

- Meet with one or two other friends regularly to share and pray together.
- Find a mentor to encourage you in your faith and make a commitment to catch up weekly or monthly.

---

11 'The Red Letters'.

- Give back to our Christian community by mentoring another person.
- Join a Bible study group.
- Try to attend church weekly, and actively contribute to your faith community.
- Allow time and space each day to hear and talk to God through prayer and reading your Bible.
- Practise hospitality regularly.

12
Redeeming Our Stories

At some point, each of us will feel that our dreams have been shattered or life has become one big insurmountable problem. Or we might grapple with thoughts in our head that torment us over and over.

Sometimes when we are in that very dark place, we think that we will never come out the other side. It swallows us up and takes over every part of our life. Some kinds of suffering are like this. We are paralysed to the point that we become isolated and are unable to reach out to other people for help. We wonder where God is and why it is happening.

It is like we enter a hiatus. A time when everything stands still and sits under a menacing shadow. The image that comes to mind is the moment when Christ was dying on the cross, 'about noon, and darkness came over the land until three in the afternoon, for the sun stopped shining' (Luke 23:44–46). Then Jesus died.

This is one way of describing what it is like to enter into the suffering of Christ. Something dies within us. This is a necessary pain, and it has no quick fix. We have to wait. There is no fast forward to Easter Sunday. We have to go through a time of nothing, a time of waiting, to prepare us for the hope of renewal and resurrection. Easter Saturday is part of this process.

This rhythm of pain, suffering, waiting, dying to self and renewal is reflected in the stories of the people I interviewed for this book. When faced with pain, each of them withdrew for a time and quietly wrestled with their life until they experienced renewal through their learning and growth about themselves and God. Reframing this, we could say it is a time of forced deconstruction and reconstruction that is necessary to make us more like Christ. The challenge is to stick with the process and come out the other side.

This need to wrestle with our stories is echoed in the work of Brene Brown,[1] social worker and researcher. She writes about the need to 'rumble' with our stories of shame, grief, failure, vulner-ability, fear, disappointment, vulnerability, perfectionism and regret. We need to capture them, write them down, and then explore their meaning. Ask ourselves important questions – for example, what do I need to learn and understand about the situ-ation, the other people in the story, and myself? The challenge as Christians is how to integrate God into the rumble so that we can make sense of our faith and life experience.

Perhaps the most confronting and encouraging part of Brené Brown's work is how she sees people as brave when they are prepared to wrestle with their stories of suffering. Living a full life means being prepared to be vulnerable enough to risk failure, mistakes and pain. To get back up when we are knocked over and try again. This difficult path is the healthiest, despite its challenges.

The tools in this book are things that I have found to help me through this process. They all rumble with story. At times, my suffering has forced me to re-evaluate what I want my life to

---

1 Brené Brown, *Rising Strong*.

be about. I have deconstructed my faith and tried to put it back together again. I have challenged my narrative and identity, and followed a different story that freed me and moved me in a new direction. I have identified destructive thinking patterns and chosen not to act on them or feed them because they are neither helpful nor true.

I could not have come through these times without precious Christian friends and family who have kept prodding me forward, and who were prepared to speak hard things into my situation. They entered the rumbling process with me. This is often how God speaks to us.

In my solitude, I have learned to listen and hear God's words in the silence.

However, the thing I turn to most when I feel overwhelmed and stuck is music. It reminds me that I am not alone. Like the Psalms, it plumbs the depths of my emotions and reorientates me to God.

It is my prayer that this book challenges you each day to look to God and have the courage to engage with the discipline of suffering. Although difficult, it will transform you so that your experience brings life, freedom, love and grace. My ultimate hope is that you are surprised by God's ability to redeem the most hopeless of situations.

I dare you to lift yourself up off the floor and move ...[2]

---

2 Foreman, J.M. 'Dare You to Move', *Learning to Breathe*, Sugar Pete Songs and Meadowgreen Music Company, 2000.

Bibliography

Australian Bureau of Statistics [ABS] (2021). 'Australia's Leading
Causes of Death, 2021', 19 October 2022, accessed 17 May 2023,
https://www.abs.gov.au/statistics/health/causes-death/causes-
death-australia/latest-release#australia-s-leading-causes-of-
death-2021

——— (2022). 'National Study of Mental Health and Wellbeing',
22 July 2022, accessed 17 May 2023, https://www.abs.gov.au/
statistics/health/mental-health/national-study-mental-health-
and-wellbeing/latest-release

——— (2014–2015). 'Mental and Behavioural Conditions', *National
Health Survey: First Results, 2014–15*, 8 December 2015, accessed
31 January 2022, https://www.abs.gov.au/ausstats/abs@.nsf/
Lookup/by%20Subject/4364.0.55.001~2014-15~Main%20Features~
Mental%20and%20behavioural%20conditions~32

Australian Institute of Health and Welfare [AIHW]. 'Deaths in
Australia', 9 June 2022, accessed 17 May 2023, https://www.aihw.
gov.au/reports/life-expectancy-death/deaths-in-australia/
contents/life-expectancy

Bessey, S. *Out of Sorts*, Howard Books, New York, 2015.

BibleProject. 'Does God Curse Generations? – Character of God E5 Q+R', 14 September 2020, https://open.spotify.com/episode/ 1ovMzYYdOjmTKneRC6V6ny

Boone, M.S., Mundy, B., Morrissey Stahl, K. & Genrich, B.E. 'Acceptance and Commitment Therapy, Functional Contextualism, and Clinical Social Work', *Journal of Human Behavior in the Social Environment*, vol. 25, 2015, pp. 643–656.

Brown, B. *Rising Strong*, Vermilion, London, 2015.

Brueggemann, W. *Spirituality of the Psalms*, Fortress Press, Minneapolis MN, 2002.

———. *Praying the Psalms: Engaging Scripture and the Life of the Spirit*, 2nd edn, Cascade Books, Eugene OR, 2007.

Bryan Smith, J. *The Good and Beautiful God*, IVP Books, Downers Grove IL, 2009.

Bunyan, J. *The Pilgrim's Progress*, Barbour Publishing Inc., Uhrichsville OH, 2010.

Ciarrochi, J., Rob, H. & Godsell, C. 'Letting a Little Nonverbal Air into the Room: Insights from Acceptance and Commitment Therapy. Part 1: Philosophical and Theoretical Underpinnings', *Journal of Rational-Emotive and Cognitive Behaviour Therapy*, vol. 23, no. 2, 2005, pp. 79–106.

Campolo, T. *Carpe Diem: Seize the Day*, Thomas Nelson, Nashville, 1994.

Conway, J. *Men in Midlife Crisis*, David Cook Publishing Co, Weston, Ontario, 1978, p. 132.

Department of Immigration and Border Protection. *Life in Australia: Australian Values and Principles*, Canberra, 2020, https://immi. homeaffairs.gov.au/support-subsite/files/life-in-australia/lia_ english_full.pdf

Flanagan, R. *The Narrow Road to the Deep North*, Vintage Books, Sydney, 2013, p. 3.

Forsyth, J.P. & Eifert, G.H. *The Mindfulness and Acceptance Workbook for Anxiety*, New Harbinger Publications Inc., Oakland CA, 2007.

Foster, R. *Life with God: A Life-transforming New Approach to Bible Reading*, Hodder, London, 2009.

Galbin, A. 'An Introduction to Social Constructionism', *Social Research Reports*, vol. 26, 2014, p. 89.

Hagberg, J.O. & Guelich, R.A. *The Critical Journey: Stages in the Life of Faith*, Sheffield Publishing Company, Wisconsin, 2005.

Hari, J. *Lost Connections*, Bloomsbury, London, 2018.

Harris, R. *The Happiness Trap*, Exisle Publishing, Sydney, 2008.

———. *The Reality Slap*, Exisle Publishing Ltd, Wollombi NSW, 2011.

Hayes, S.C. 'Acceptance and Commitment Therapy, Relational Frame Theory, and the Third Wave of Behavioral and Cognitive Therapies', *Behavior Therapy*, vol. 47, 2016, pp. 869–885.

———, Barnes-Holmes, D. & Wilson, K.G. 'Contextual Behavioural Science: Creating a Science More Adequate to the Challenge of the Human Condition', *Journal of Contextual Behavioural Science*, vol. 1, 2012, pp. 1–16.

Herbert, J.D. & Padovani, F. 'Contextualism, Psychological Science, and the Question of Ontology', *Journal of Contextual Behavioural Science*, vol. 4, 2015, pp. 225–230.

Hinn, C. *God, Greed and the (Prosperity) Gospel: How Truth Overwhelms a Life Built on Lies*, Zondervan, Grand Rapids MI, 2019.

Hurnard, H. *Hinds' Feet on High Places*, Tyndale House Publishers, London UK, 1975.

Jacobson, K. 'Through the Pistol Smoke Dimly: Psalm 23 In Contemporary Film and Song 2009', *SBL Forum*, January 2009, https://www.sbl-site.org/publications/article.aspx?articleId=796

Johnstone, M. *Quiet the Mind: An Illustrated Guide on How to Meditate*, Pan Macmillan Australia, Sydney, 2013.

Jones, R. *Is This It? The Difference Jesus Makes to that 'Where-is-my-life-going-I-hate-my-job-I-have-no-real-friends-Is-God-even-There-Will-I-end-up-alone-I-wish-I-was-back-at-school-Will-this-ever-feel-like-home-Am-I-failing-at-life' Feeling*, The Good Book Company, London, 2019.

Kaplan, H.I. & Sadock, B.J. *Synopsis of Psychiatry*, Lippincott Williams & Wilkins, Balitmore MD, 1998.

McMinn, M. *The Science of Virtue: Why Positive Psychology Matters to the Church*, Brazos Press, Grand Rapids MI, 2017.

Moltmann, J. *The Source of Life*, SCM Press Ltd, London, 1997.

———. *The Crucified God*, Fortress Press, Minneapolis, 2015.

Polk, K. 'The ACT Matrix', Association for Contextual Behavioural Science, https://contextualscience.org/act_matrix

Rohr, R. *The Naked Now*, Crossroad Publishing Company, New York, 2015.

Roth, V. *Divergent*, Harper Collins, London, 2011.

———. *Insurgent*, Harper Collins, London, 2012.

———. *Allegiant*, Harper Collins, London, 2013.

Sales, L. *Any Ordinary Day: Blindsides, Resilience and What Happens After the Worst Day of Your Life*, Hamish Hamilton, London, 2018.

Seligman, M. *Flourish: A Visionary New Understanding of Happiness and Well-being*, William Heinemann, Sydney, 2011.

St John of the Cross, 'Dark Night of the Soul', in *The Top 7 Catholic Classics: On Loving God, The Cloud of Unknowing, Dialogue of Saint Catherine of Siena, The Imitation of Christ, Interior Castle, Dark Night of the Soul, The Practice of the Presence of God*, Kindle edn, Amazon Digital Services, London, 2012.

Shorrocks, A., Davies, J., & Lluberas, R. *Global Wealth Databook 2018*, Credit Suisse, October 2018, https://en.m.wikipedia.org/wiki/List_of_countries_by_wealth_per_adult

Stoddard, J.A. & Fari, N. *The Big Book of ACT Metaphors*, New Harbinger Publications, Oakland CA, 2014.

'The Red Letters', Red Letter Christians, https://www.redletterchristians.org/the-red-letters/

Thompson, K. *Christ-Centred Mindfulness: Connection to Self and God*, Acorn Press, Sydney, 2018.

Twohig, M.P. 'Introduction: The Basics of Acceptance and Commitment Therapy', *Cognitive and Behavioural Practice*, vol. 19, 2012, pp. 499–507.

Vilardaga, R., Hayes, S.C. & Schelin, L. 'Philosophical, theoretical and empirical foundations of Acceptance and Commitment Therapy', *Anuario de Psicologia*, vol. 38, 2007, pp. 117–128.

Welborn, A. 'Suscipe, the Radical Prayer', IgnatianSpirituality.com, n.d., https://www.ignatianspirituality.com/ignatian-prayer/prayers-by-st-ignatius-and-others/suscipe-the-radical-prayer/

White, M. & Epston, D. *Narrative Means to Therapeutic Ends*, WW Norton & Company, New York, 1990.

Wiesel, E. 'US News and World Report', 27 October 1986. In Susan Ratcliffe, Oxford Dictionary of Quotations by Subject, Oxford University Press, Oxford, 2010, p. 249.

Willard, D. *Hearing God*, IVP, Downers Grove IL, 2012.

————. *The Spirit of the Disciplines: Understanding How God Changes Lives*, Harper Collins, New York, 1991.

Wilson, A. 'Does God Give and Take Away?', Thinktheology.co.uk, 22 February 2012, https://thinktheology.co.uk/blog/article/does-god-give-and-take-away

Witherington, B. 'Good Grief – What Does It Look Like?', 24 January 2012, https://www.patheos.com/blogs/bibleand culture/2012/01/24/good-grief-soundings-part-one/

World Health Organisation. 'Mental Health: Strengthening Our Response', 2018, https://www.who.int/news-room/fact-sheets/detail/mental-health-strengthening-our-response

Wright, N.T. *Paul: A Biography*, Harper One, San Francisco, 2018.

Young, W.P., Jacobsen, W. & Cummings, B. *The Shack: Where Tragedy Confronts Eternity*, Windblown Media, Newbury Park CA, 2007.

About the Author

Dr Katherine Thompson BA, BAppSci (Hons), BTh, BSW, PhD, is an Accredited Mental Health Social Worker and a Member of the Australian College of Social Workers. She works in the area of mental health as a therapist, lecturer, author and researcher.

Katherine is passionate about supporting young people with mental health challenges to live their best lives, and seeks to encourage people in ministry to thrive in their role. She currently divides her time between her work as a mental health social worker and therapist in private practice, and as a Senior Lecturer in Mental Health and Wellbeing at the Melbourne School of Theology and Eastern College Australia.

She has published in the areas of youth mental health, Christ-centred mindfulness, and cross-cultural mission. In 2019, her book *Christ-Centred Mindfulness: Connection to Self and God* was announced the co-winner of the Martin Institute for Christianity and Culture and Dallas Willard Research Center Book Award.

Katherine has her own private practice with a focus on young people aged 12–25 years, as well as ministry and mission staff. She is most content when outside in nature connecting to God in quietness through his creation.

Other books by Katherine Thompson

Christ-Centred Mindfulness: Connection to Self and God

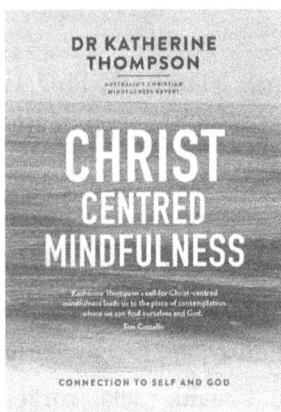

Does mindfulness improve our wellbeing?
Can it be practised within a Christian worldview?
Can it be Christ-Centred?
Yes.

In the award-winning *Christ-Centred Mindfulness*, leading academic and experienced mental health worker Dr Katherine Thompson addresses these questions and draws on the rich Christian tradition to present Christian mindfulness exercises that help us slow down, connect to what is happening inside ourselves and make space to listen for God's guidance in everyday life.

Whether you're a Christian who is curious about mindfulness practice and its benefits, or you work in a counselling profession and are trying to sort through your own approach to mindfulness-based therapies, this book is for you.

Breathe and *Still*

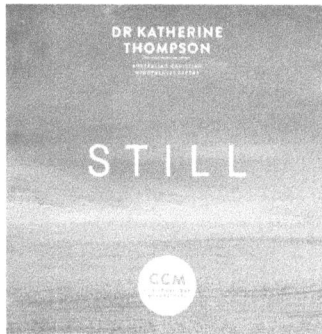

Christ-centred mindfulness teaches us to live in the present moment with a continual connection to God and an awareness of our inner world. It is a pathway to peace, transformation and a deeper relationship with God. At its most basic, it encourages us to stop, disconnect from distractions and busyness, and breathe.

The practice of Christ-centred mindfulness helps us to become better at being silent and to listen to God. The more we are prepared to do this, the easier it is to hear God's voice directing us deep within our being.

The exercises in these books are designed to provoke your thinking and discipline you to take time out of your busy life to listen to God.

For more information about these books, visit www.acornpress.net.au

www.ingramcontent.com/pod-product-compliance
Lightning Source LLC
Chambersburg PA
CBHW070802280326
41934CB00012B/3027